Praise for

THE *GIFTS* OF WRITING

"In the ways that Julia Cameron and Mark Nepo have revealed the sacred possibilities that lie within the written word, and shown them to be mirrors of our soul and sign posts to an inner joy, so too does Hope Koppelman take us on a journey with her debut book, *The Gifts of Writing*. Masterfully written with love and a true passion for the mystery of our ability to create."

—Mike Dooley, *NY Times* bestselling author of *Infinite Possibilities*

"Words have incredible power—to heal and transform us. They help us feel and face things, enliven and stir things within us. They are an expression of our human art; who we are. Hope Koppelman is an art whisperer who makes art of her prose. Born surrounded by art and artists—it is the language she speaks. For years, she has made art of the work of others—and finally, she births her own. *The Gifts of Writing* is the soul kiss to the art and the artist within each of us that we have all been waiting for. It is our permission slip and our prayer to step in and claim our inner writer—and to get our words out."

—Kristen Noel, editor-in-chief *Best Self Magazine*

"Hope Koppelman's heart and vision shine through this rare and inspiring guide to writing from the soul. I am deeply inspired by the sensitivity that Hope masterfully displays in her many well-thought-out and highly stimulating perspectives on using writing as a tool to deliver healing and transformation not just to readers, but to the writer as well. If you are a writer or are thinking about becoming one, this will serve as a valued and trustworthy companion as you share your most cherished ideas, and grow through the process. Highly recommended!"

—Alan Cohen, award-winning author of *A Deep Breath of Life*

THE *GIFTS* OF WRITING

TUT PUBLISHING
an imprint of TUT Enterprises, Inc.
Orlando, Florida
tut.com

10 9 8 7 6 5 4 3 2

Printed in the United States of America

Trade Paperback ISBN: 978-1-7352-5950-5
e-Book ISBN: 978-1-7352-5951-2

Library of Congress Control Number: 2020911656

Designed by Gina Tyquiengco

THE *gifts* OF WRITING

Exploring the Mystery, Magic, and
Wonder of the Creative Process

HOPE KOPPELMAN

TUT PUBLISHING

ORLANDO

To Mom,
Know your self
without the sea,
only then can you
know your self
with the ocean.

CONTENTS

An Invitation

The gifts that writing offers us are endless in nature.
I am constantly discovering new gifts each time
I sit down to write. It never ceases to amaze me.

If there is one thing I hope to share with you
through this book, it's the realization, or better yet
the knowing, that these gifts exist within you.

They are already there, waiting for you,
ready for you, hoping you will have the curiosity
and the courage to go looking for them.

Everything you could ever hope to discover
or understand or make peace with or let go of
or grow into is already a part of you, just waiting
for you to pick up a pen and come find it.

It's all there for you.

Listening

Writing asks us to listen.
It asks us to feel.
It asks us to be present.
It asks us to be quiet.
It asks us to be still.

Writing as a Form of Meditation

Writing asks us to listen instead of speak. It asks us to feel. It asks us to be present. It asks us to be quiet. It asks us to be still. These are the same characteristics of meditation, and when we honor what writing is asking of us, then writing does become a form of meditation. I have always regarded writing as a form of "working meditation," and I've found that when I approach it in this way, I am more gentle and forgiving with myself. I release my expectations. I don't force anything. I show up with an open mind and an open heart, ready to see where the practice will lead me each day. There is an element of trust involved, a turning over of sorts to that which is unknown to us. Are we willing to surrender control? Are we willing to release our expectations? Are we willing to trust our intuition? That is the writer's practice.

Creating and Cultivating Inspiration

Taking a hike.

Sitting beneath a tree.

Watching the ripples in a lake.

Looking up at the stars at night.

Laying in the grass on a summer day.

These moments of quiet connection between ourselves and our world create a bond that inspiration can flow through. When we are ready—ready to listen, ready to feel, ready to see, and ready to receive in this way, the right words and ideas will find us. There is a collaboration that takes place, as in every relationship. We create the space, the quiet, the solitude, to be present with the world around us, and from that point the world opens up to us and speaks.

An Exchange of Trust

Writing has many of the same properties as prayer. It's a complete turning over of ourselves to a greater power. When we pray, we are stepping into our vulnerability. We are opening up from the inside and allowing ourselves to be heard. It is a moment of truth; an exchange of trust. Writing is also an exchange of trust. We come to the page like we come to pray—vulnerable, open, honest, a little scared at times. We may never be fully prepared or know exactly what's going to happen once we get there. We just know that we must show up and speak our truth. That is our part in the partnership. Deep down, in every cell of our being, we know that if we do our part to show up with faith, then the greater power at hand will do its part to meet us there with gifts of inspiration and insight.

Summoning Inspiration

The words I write almost always follow some sort of action on my part to summon them. Either sitting down at the computer or journaling in my notebook or quietly contemplating the world around me. It starts with a willingness to observe and listen. That's when inspiration comes—when we are fully engaged in the present moment and making ourselves available to receive.

Here's how the process unfolds for me:

1. I plan in advance. I decide when I will write, and I make it a priority. Sometimes that means going to bed by a certain time, waking up earlier than usual, or rearranging my schedule. It starts with making a commitment to myself that I know I will keep.

2. I make a cup of tea or maca latte* and go to my writing spot. Sometimes on my back porch. Sometimes in front of my computer. Sometimes at the coffee shop around the corner. Wherever I feel compelled to start on that particular day is where I go (and where I start is rarely where I finish).

* For recipe, see page 237.

3. I relax into where I am. I don't expect anything. I'm not there for any reason, except to be present and observe what unfolds. I know that by quieting my mind and listening, I am opening myself to receive. That's all I focus on.

4. I start writing, without knowing where it will lead; without any idea of what I will write about. I just go. And as I go, ideas start to unfold and stories start to take form.

5. I stay with it. I continue to write for as long as it feels good, until I'm ready to stop and move on to the next thing.

6. Then I start the process all over again.

Receiving the Truth

I have found that by getting quiet and listening, the truth always comes to me—whether through writing or meditation or prayer. If I can quiet my thoughts, close my eyes, and breathe for a few minutes, finding the space that exists in-between all the busyness and commotion, then I can receive the truth from some deeper place. It comes swiftly and easily, but only when we first create the space for it. When we create a sense of ease within ourselves, then the truth can flow more easily, bringing with it insights, ideas, and illumination. With practice, we can carry this feeling of ease with us wherever we go, whether we are sitting at home writing or out in the world living our lives, availing ourselves to truth all the time.

The Inner Witness

The part of us that is always listening, always observing, always taking in—that is our inner witness. Writers and artists especially are in an ongoing conversation with their inner witness, because that is the part of themselves that is always on the lookout for new ideas, new insights, and new discoveries. The inner witness asks us to open our eyes, listen deeply, watch the world attentively, ask questions, observe with an open mind, and feel what's taking place. The inner witness works on a subconscious level, whether we are aware of it or not, drawing from the world around us and storing the information it finds for later use. We are always collecting information, without even looking for it. Our inner witness does it for us. We simply have to step out into the world, and our inner witness steps out with us; sit at our desk to work, and our inner witness delivers ideas; listen and observe, and our inner witness receives the insights the world is offering us.

Listening to Our Intuition

Whenever I travel alone to new places, I ask my intuition to guide me. I listen to it each step of the way, check in with it, get quiet enough to hear what it is telling me. *Should I go this way or that way?* I ask it. A gentle leaning one way or the other is all I need to feel; a subtle pull that leads me to take one step after another down this street or that alleyway, to turn left or go straight or turn right. There is no logic behind it. It's just a subtle pull, so subtle I could easily miss it if I weren't paying attention and listening closely for the feeling to tell me which way to go.

Writing relies on the same intuitive sense. It's not through thinking but through feeling that we are able to listen to where the words want to lead us. It's through getting quiet and listening that we are able to feel the direction the words want to take. Just like learning to trust our intuition when we travel, we learn to trust our intuition while we write, knowing that it will lead us in the right direction and to places we aren't expecting to find.

Wake, Pray, Work

A dear friend of mine once said that we would be wise to start each day in this order: wake, pray, work. This way, we always put our connection to the divine ahead of everything else that we do. I believe she is right. Even if you're not religious, even if you don't consider yourself a spiritual person, there is a checking in with oneself that can occur before the work begins. A moment for getting quiet, becoming present, and putting the call out to all the elements of the universe that *it's time to work!* If we just charge ahead into the work, we risk forfeiting this moment of connection; this moment of sacred communication that happens when we understand that we are not alone in the creative process. Writing is not as solitary as most people think. We are working in tandem with the universe and all the elements of the earth. We are collaborating with something greater than ourselves—the powerful unknown—to create what has never been created before.

The Vibrations of Life

I remember, as a small child, resting my head upon my mother's breast and listening to her heartbeat. In those moments, I felt empty of thoughts, empty of words, empty of everything except the vibration of her heartbeat speaking to mine, filling me with a sense of all I needed— safety, security, comfort, love.

I believe the truth is carried through vibrations (energies) that exist at the center of everything. It's what existed before there were words, before our translation of the world began, and it's what exists now, billions of years later. As writers and artists, we are faced with the task of translating these vibrations, these energies, into tangible form through the narrow channels of language and music and art. If we are successful, we might capture the essence of that truth, a glimmer of it, a reflection that will offer people a hint of what's really there. If we even come close it is a great accomplishment, perhaps "mastery" at its finest—to give someone a peek, a window at most, into something so spectacular, so magnificent, it cannot possibly fit into our human understanding of it.

Going Deeply into the Quiet

We owe ourselves dedicated time to being alone. Time that's devoted to getting to know ourselves and deepening our relationship with ourselves. If we are always rushing to work, to visit friends, to pick up our children, to run errands, then the focus of our energy isn't on the stillness that is so essential for writing. It's up to us to create the space in our lives where it is safe to cultivate stillness; where it is safe to explore our thoughts and feelings; where it is safe to enter into a state of deeper resonance with life.

Set aside time for deep reflection once a day or several times a week. Setting aside time on a regular basis will condition you to return to it, and you'll begin to notice that this becomes precious, sacred time. *What ever would I do without it...* you might wonder. This time for deep reflection sets the foundation for your writing practice. It prepares you for writing deeply when the opportunity comes. Whether you're folding laundry or cooking dinner or taking a walk outside, when you're alone, there is time to reflect. Seek out this time and know that it's making possible an even deeper writing practice.

An Essential Element of Writing

One of the most essential elements of writing is listening. Learning to quiet the mind, quiet the effort, quiet the expectations—and find stillness. When we allow ourselves to be still and listen, we are able to feel what we are writing and bring truth to what we are saying. My process of listening looks like this: I find a quiet spot, usually outside in a rocking chair on my back porch or in a cozy corner of my living room. I bring pen and paper. Then I begin to feel. If I'm outside, I feel the sun's warm touch on my face. I listen to the breeze. I become part of the stillness. I never know what's going to come. I let go of any desire to write well. I want the words to flow freely. I want them to come without force, and they do, when I am listening. This slow process of listen, pause, write… listen, pause, write… reminds me that the speed of writing isn't important. Listening is what matters.

Honoring the Present Moment

For many years I have been practicing yoga several times a week. One of the first lessons I learned (and continue to learn over and over again) is that our strength as practitioners comes from our ability to be fully present and connect to the moment we are in. As soon as we start to think about which posture comes next, we lose our connection to the present moment—our mind starts to wander, our breath becomes shallow, our inner-focus falters. The posture we are in (warrior, downward dog, fierce pose, boat) becomes more challenging to hold because it isn't supported by the breath anymore. It's our ability to come fully into the present moment and breathe deeply into that space which allows us to get the most benefit from where we are.

The same is true of writing. When we write, the truth of a word, every word, depends on our ability to quiet the mind of future thoughts. It is then that we are fully prepared to listen, as we would listen to a lover or a friend who is confiding a deeply personal secret to us. It is then that we can give our undivided attention, release our expectations, drop our judgments, and hear the truth. We will not hear it if we are thinking about what comes next.

To honor the work means to honor the moment. Let go of every competing thought that interferes with it, and recognize that being present and listening is enough.

The Beauty of Practice

I have devoted much of my life to the practice of practice. Learning to be in the present moment; to relish the simple things like waking up each morning, making a cup of tea, taking a walk outside, picking out my clothes for the day. All that we do has the potential to become a practice, bringing us deeper into the present moment and making us more aware of ourselves and the world around us.

There are the obvious practices we think of: the practice of writing, the practice of yoga, the practice of meditation. But then there are the practices we may not think of as often: the practice of listening, the practice of compassion, the practice of awareness. *Each moment is an opportunity to practice something that will add to us.* If we are stuck in traffic and late for work, it's an opportunity to practice slowing down and surrendering control. If we are feeling sad or confused or overwhelmed, it's an opportunity to practice treating ourselves gently with compassion. If we are stepping into the creative space for the first time in a long time, it's an opportunity to practice releasing our expectations and trusting ourselves. All of life is a practice, and each moment is an opportunity to deepen our commitment to it.

Starting the Day with Purpose

When we start the day feeling connected to what we love, whether it's writing or meditating or taking a walk outside, it's easier to stay connected to that feeling all day long. What we choose to empower first thing when we wake up sets the pace for our entire day to follow. This is why each morning, just as the sun is coming up, I like to walk around the lake behind my house. I walk slowly, writing in my notebook along the way, smiling to strangers who are finding their own moment of connection with the world, like me. I take this time to listen and observe and write. I listen to the sounds of nature around me. I become aware of what I'm feeling. I invite gratitude and peace and love to accompany me as I walk, knowing that these are the feelings I'm choosing to guide me through my day.

When you wake up each morning, let the first thing you do be something you love, something that calls in the feelings you want to guide you through your day. It might be as simple as sitting on your porch and sipping a cup of tea or taking a walk around the block or journaling for fifteen minutes. When you start the day with purpose—doing something you love—*all else falls into place.*

Practice: Slow Walking

I like to start my mornings with a slow walking exercise. I wake up early, when the birds are chirping and the rest of the world is still asleep, and I walk around the lake behind my house. I carry pen and paper, and walk slowly. I have no thoughts of where I'm going to end up, or how I'm going to get there; I walk only for the experience of being where I am. My intention is not to create. My intention is to be present and feel connected to the world around me. If I write, that's fine. If not, that's fine, too. This exercise is about coming into the present moment without any expectations. I invite you to try it:

Bring a notebook with you.
If nothing gets written, that's fine.
Walk for the sake of walking, not writing.
Allow yourself to be fully present without expectations.
Observe the world around you without judgment.
Take it in, absorb it, breathe it.
If you feel moved to write, then write.
If not, just listen.

Showing Up

Being an artist is simply about
spending a little bit of time, each day,
giving voice to what you love.

Giving Voice to What We Love

Being an artist is simply about spending a little bit of time, each day, giving voice to what you love. That's all it takes. The happiest artists I know are the ones in motion—doing the work they love, showing up to it consistently, engaging with it on a regular basis, and continuously deepening their relationship with it. It's as simple as doing the work they love each day, for ten minutes or half an hour. Just long enough to touch it and feel it and remember why they love it. That small reminder is all we need to keep us coming back, day after day, for the rest of our lives.

Choosing a Time to Write

I have always loved to write in the mornings. Life rolls in at a softer pace. The burdens of the day have yet to impose themselves on us. Our lives are still simple—wake up, make tea, settle in to write. There isn't a running to-do list that's been growing longer with every hour of the day. There is an innocence to the world in its quiet state. I wonder sometimes, if life were comprised solely of mornings, would the world be a more peaceful place? This is the time of day that resonates with me the most. This is when I love to sit down at the computer with my tea and dive into the work. Find a time of day to write that resonates with you. Form a relationship with it. Learn its secrets. What makes it special? What do you love about that magical hour?

Setting the Space

If you knew you wanted to climb Mount Everest, you would have to prepare in advance—do lots of research, buy the equipment you need, set a training schedule, condition yourself. There's a lot that goes into it, before you ever make it to the mountain. The same is true of writing. We can't just wait for inspiration to strike before we take action. We have to set the space for our practice in advance, and then show up and fill it with our presence.

I set the space for writing by making the room where I write feel sacred. I clear my desk, everything except for my computer, a small bamboo plant that I place in the corner, a couple of candles, an incense holder. I clear away all the clutter and leave only the things I want to see each day. Then I make a plan. I decide, in advance, that I will wake up the next morning at 7 a.m. (not every morning for the rest of my life, just tomorrow morning). I set my alarm. I get up. I make a cup of tea. I light a few candles and a stick of incense. Then I sit down at my desk to write.

Can you try it? Can you devote one day, perhaps even today, to setting the space for your writing practice?

Opening Ourselves to Receive

Inspiration is like anything you open yourself to receive—healing, happiness, clarity, love. When you make the decision to bring it into your life and you stand poised to receive it, it will show up. *Your job is to decide what you want, and then make yourself available to it.* You wouldn't decide you were ready to fall in love and then hibernate indoors for the rest of your life. You would put yourself out into the world where love can reach you. You would show up to life each day with open eyes and an open heart and an attitude of vulnerability, so that the moment you sensed the presence of love, you would recognize it. Show up to writing the same way, with an attitude that's open and vulnerable, ready to receive the gifts that will come. There is a surrendering that occurs once you decide, truly decide, you are ready to welcome change into your life. From that moment on, there is no going back, there is no waiting around, there is no "pause" button you can press to slow the tides.

Where Creativity Starts

The moment we start writing words on the page in front of us or applying paint to the canvas, we begin to see more clearly. That's when we realize what we think, what we feel, and what our ideas are. It's only after we think them, feel them, say them, write them, paint them, sing them, that they come fully into focus. I rarely have an idea and think to myself, "I have to write about that!" I'm afraid many people think that's where creativity starts—with a great idea. So they wait for it, and they wait for it, and they wait for it, and it never comes. They say things like, "I don't know what to create," "I'm not inspired," "I don't have any ideas." If only they knew, that feeling of uncertainty and unknowing is *exactly* where creativity starts. So the next time you think to yourself, "I don't have any ideas," or "I don't know where to start," realize that you're in a place of unknowing, and that's exactly where you belong.

A Settling Period Early On

My relationship with writing has often resembled a marriage. In the beginning, I had to learn to work together and live together with it constructively. It was a time of getting to know myself, as my level of intimacy with the work grew deeper. I knew that I loved writing, but I still didn't know who I was as a writer. I didn't know if I was more suited to writing poetry or prose or fiction or non-fiction. I didn't know if I preferred to write longhand or at the computer. I didn't know what time of day I preferred to write or where I did my best writing. It was a settling period. I was settling into my identity as a writer, and as I did, these unknowns became clearer.

There is a settling period for all artists, when we are just starting out and putting down roots. It feels foreign, like we are unsure of everything we are doing. Do it anyway. Trust that the instincts you feel are right. There is something beautiful about the beginning when we are settling into a new identity for the first time. There is a softness to our steps, a gentleness to our approach. We are more willing to take our time and go slow.

The Answers Are in the Work

Your questions will be answered once you begin to create the work. *What kind of writer am I? What story do I want to tell? What message do I want to share with the world?* We know little of these things at the start. We know little until we are deep into the writing process and can look back at what we have written and learn from the work. The work will show you "what" and "why" and "who" and "how." The answers will become clear once you get started.

Finding Our Way into the Practice

I once watched a young man walk into a yoga studio, sit down on his yoga mat, pop open a can of Red Bull energy drink and chug the entire thing before belching loudly for everyone to hear. At first I thought, *this guy doesn't belong in a yoga class... he won't last longer than a day.* But then I remembered, midway through my judgment, that most people don't start yoga as mindful and conscientious practitioners; most people become mindful and conscientious practitioners after years of practicing yoga.

There is no wrong way into a practice—whether it be the practice of yoga or meditation or writing or rock-climbing. The term "practice" implies that we are there to learn and grow from our experience. We don't begin as experts, and for as long as we continue to approach the work as a practice we will never become experts. You can show up to a yoga class with a leather yoga mat and designer yoga pants, and still be doing it right, as long as you are attempting to find your way into the practice. You can show up to writing with the TV blaring, hungover from the night before, and still be doing it right, as long as you are attempting to find your way into the practice. There is no wrong way in, because once you are in, it doesn't matter how you got there.

Making It Easier for Ourselves

A dear friend of mine put her three small children into music lessons so that they could learn to play an instrument of their choosing. When she picked them up from their first lesson, their music teacher pulled her aside and whispered into her ear, "When you get home, don't put the instruments in their cases or the children will never want to take them out. Leave them out of their cases, in the middle of the living room, and they'll be more inclined to practice each day."

Isn't this true of all the things we want to grow and cultivate in our lives? To deepen our practice of any kind, half the challenge is making it easier for ourselves. If you want to start writing, carry a notebook with you everywhere you go, so it's always nearby. If you want to start painting, set up your easel and paints in the middle of your bedroom or wherever it will become the biggest nuisance if you don't do something about it. The creative work we're doing should always be at the forefront of our lives, never farther than an arm's length away, so that we can reach for it and find it anytime.

The Simple Task of Writing

Most of the work we do as writers is not divinely inspired work. It's sitting down under imperfect conditions and doing the task in front of us. Throwing away the crummy work. Tweaking and finessing the semi-crummy work that might have a chance at becoming better. Moving things around on the page, and then moving them around some more.

Think of writing the way you think of brushing your teeth or taking a shower or eating breakfast. Those things don't inspire you. They don't make your heart sing every time you do them. You don't stress about them or wait for inspiration to strike. *You do them because you know they're tasks that need to get done, for your health, your happiness, your well-being, your sanity.* Treat writing as a task you need to do in order to live sanely. Do it, get it done, and move on to the next thing. Make it a simple routine that you sit down to without too much forethought or planning.

The Dangers of Inspiration

I am fully aware that if I talk about inspiration, I will begin to believe in it. And if I believe in it, I will begin to act like it exists. And if I act like it exists, I will wait for inspiration to strike before I take action; I will wait for an idea to materialize before I begin. So I choose not to talk about inspiration, because I don't like to wait. I prefer to write.

Making Time to Write

There is rarely enough time in the day to write as much as one would like. The list of responsibilities that compete for our attention grows longer by the hour, and by the minute on some days, so finding time to write can seem impossible. This is why we must make time to write instead, because we will never find it by waiting for it to appear. If we want it, we have to create it by saying, "No, not right now," to our other responsibilities. "No, not right now," to packing our child's lunch for school. "No, not right now," to the pile of dirty laundry on the floor. "No, not right now," to our best friend who wants to stop over after work. "No, not right now," to the emails and phone calls we haven't responded to. "No, not right now," to our favorite TV shows. *Sometimes we have to say no to five things in order to say yes to one that really matters.* For many of us, this is the only way we can turn our attention to writing and give it the time and energy it deserves.

Falling in Love with Imperfection

What are you waiting for? What do you believe needs to happen before you can start writing? Is there some criteria you haven't met? Do you need a college degree or a Masters in comparative literature? Is there a time constraint? Perhaps you have children to raise or a career that demands your full attention?

The one fatal flaw that artists must be careful not to make is believing that everything has to be perfect before the work can begin. The truth is, nothing has to be perfect before the work can begin. If you want to be an artist and spend your life creating, then learn to enjoy creating under imperfect circumstances—when you don't have enough time and you don't have enough quiet and you don't have the adequate space that you need. *Find the beauty in the imperfection and create anyway.* An important part of becoming a writer (or anything for that matter) is learning to fall in love with the process and what it brings. The people who only love certain parts of the process, the inspired moments when writing comes easy or what results in the end, won't last long before their enthusiasm wanes. But the people who learn to love all of it, the inspired moments and the challenging moments alike, and continue to push on regardless of where they find themselves, will discover a lifetime of happiness.

The Yearning to Write

I have learned to be grateful for the busyness of my life. The moments when I feel called to write but have to turn my back on it to get to work on time or practice yoga or cook dinner. If it weren't for the yearning to write, the eagerness to find time to do it, I don't know if I would feel half as accomplished as I do sitting down to it. I wonder sometimes, if it weren't for the busyness in my life, if I had all the time I needed to write, would I grow tired of it? There's something wonderful about having to yearn to write, having to earn every moment you spend with it.

Showing up to the Work

Some days we just skim the surface with our writing. We don't go very deep. We add a comma here or a semi-colon there. Perhaps, if we're lucky, a good sentence is born out of a weak paragraph. I used to think that writing on these days was a waste of time; that if I didn't feel inspired, there was no point in sitting down to write. Fortunately, I didn't listen to those thoughts, because it would have meant the end of my journey to becoming a writer. It was only through the process of sitting down to write under every psychological state of mind and emotional state of being that I discovered the writing doesn't discriminate; it doesn't even care what our state of mind or being is—*all of it is energy that can be used to fuel our work.* The worst-case scenario is that we show up to write, and we don't write well. That's okay, because we're still showing up, we're still making progress, we're still stepping into the role of a writer, and we're still one step closer than we were the day before. The best-case scenario is all of the above, and we write well.

Training the Muscle

Writing is a muscle we have to strengthen and develop. When I sit down to write after spending months away from it, I'm exhausted after the first hour of writing. I have to go and take a nap. I can't keep my eyes open, because I'm not used to the intense focus and concentration that goes into it. But when I have been writing consistently and my writing muscle is strong, I can sit down to it for hours without losing focus. I lose track of time. The phone rings, and I don't reach for it. Someone knocks on the front door, and I don't answer it. Lunch time comes and goes, and I keep on writing, without so much as a growl from my empty stomach. The difference between a trained muscle and an untrained muscle is exercise, practice. The more we use it, the stronger it becomes, the better it works.

The Easy Way In

I have a friend who plays the fiddle, and each day she practices the same sequence of musical exercises she practiced the day before. Day after day, year after year, she starts her practice with the same simple notes. She does this because it's an easy way in to the creative process. It doesn't require a lot of effort—she can practically play the notes in her sleep. She can play them whether she's having a good day or a bad day, whether she's in the mood to practice or not. I admire her willingness to start small, knowing that it will lead her to greater things. By the end of the day, she's often deep in the creative flow—writing new songs and improvising with new lyrics and melodies. I encourage all artists to start with the easy way in. Start with a simple exercise or writing prompt to get going. Write a few questions on a sheet of paper and tear them up into tiny pieces and put them in a bowl. Where do you want to travel? What's on your mind? What are you grateful for? Then choose a new one at random to write about. It doesn't matter what you start writing about; you'll find your way to the important stuff once you begin.

The Magic of Creativity

Writing is not a science. It is not something we can teach to ourselves through a series of rules or formulas. There aren't specific steps to take as there are in mathematics. Writing calls upon something deeper, something that will always remain a mystery, no matter how many books we write during our lifetime. This is true of music and art and anything that comes alive through creativity. We could spend our entire lives trying to figure it out, but there is something magical in creativity that we will never fully understand. There is something greater at play.

For this reason, it is our faith in the unknown that leads us to discover what we are capable of creatively. It is our faith in the unknown that opens us up to a sea of possibilities—a sea that is constantly expanding and taking us deeper into the depths of ourselves. However, it is our actions that bring faith to life. We have to show up in a practical sense: sit at the computer and write; journal in our notebooks; set aside time to be still and listen. The magic happens when faith is met by practicality, when dreaming is met by action. We may not know what the magic is or where it comes from, but we do know how to invoke it.

Gathering Courage

A friend of mine spent several years traveling around the world. Backpacking through Europe, Asia, Australia, and working odd jobs along the way—tending to people's organic gardens, collecting eggs from their chicken coops, serving gyros at local fairs. He's one of those fearless people who wants to go everywhere and try everything once. So, naturally, I was surprised to learn that on his first solo trip outside the United States he was terrified—so terrified that he didn't leave his hotel for several days. He sat inside his tiny room, looking out the window at all the people walking by, speaking a language he didn't speak, while slowly gathering up his courage to venture out into the unknown. Eventually, he did get up the courage, and he fell in love with the world he found.

His experience reminds me that we only ever have to take one small step at a time. We just have to get ourselves into the space from which writing or traveling or anything else we want to do can come more easily. Step one is simple: go to the space. *Step two is trust that courage and inspiration and whatever else you need will meet you there and guide you the rest of the way.* Give yourself time. Show up each day without forcing anything to come from it,

and, eventually, there will come a moment when you will
gather up the courage to pick up your pen and write.

Gradual Change

Can you fall in love with change on a microscopic level? If so, you'll learn to notice and appreciate the progress you make. Change happens slowly in writing—a tweak to a sentence, adding a comma, moving a paragraph. We take two steps forward and one step back. Then again, who's to say that even our steps back aren't progress if we're learning from them. Change is gradual, especially when we are watching it unfold through the creative process. That's why it's so important to recognize even the smallest changes as progress, because, whether we take two steps forward or one back, we are taking steps, and every step matters.

Some days I write, and little gets accomplished. Some days I meditate, and I can't stop the thoughts running through my head. Some days I wake up feeling like everything around me is the same as it was the day before. And you know what? All of it is progress, because I am writing, I am meditating, and I am waking up. I am showing up to the world each day and moving with my desires. Sometimes I move forward, sometimes I move backward, and sometimes I move in circles... but I always move, and a step in any direction is still a step.

The Dance

There is a beautiful relationship between the writer and spirit (call it what you will: inspiration, magic, God). We summon it each time we show up to create.

We take the first step, and spirit meets us.

We listen, and spirit speaks.

We open, and spirit fills us.

We write, and spirit guides us.

It is a dance that grows deeper with each move we make.

It's All Progress

The very act of sitting down to write is progress, even if nothing happens after that. Don't measure progress by what you see in front of you: word counts, pages written, chapters finished, books published. These are superficial forms of measurement that don't take into account the rest of the work you're doing. You are making progress every time you take one step closer to being a writer: every time you sit down to write, every time you put pen to paper, every time you read a book that you love, every time you journal, every time you think of a new idea, every time you write when you're inspired, every time you write when you're uninspired. *It's all progress.* So be gentle with yourself, and know that progress is happening all the time, even when it doesn't appear to amount to much right away.

Putting a Call Out to the Universe

I recently started a ritual of asking the universe for what I need, each night before I go to sleep. Sometimes I ask for clarity. Sometimes I ask for guidance. Sometimes I ask for comfort. Sometimes I simply say: *If there is anything I need to receive, please deliver it to me in my sleep.* I've been amazed to discover that almost always that which I ask for comes to me. I awake with a dream or an insight or a clarifying thought that reveals what I was hoping to receive. It's not always this direct though; sometimes I awake in the morning without any such realization, but I have the distinct feeling that I received what I needed subconsciously. I know that it doesn't matter whether I'm fully aware of having received it or not, because it's already a part of me, and it will become apparent soon enough.

The wonderful thing is that now this has begun to happen even without my asking for it—as if putting a call out to the universe as often as I did has made clear what I'm looking for, and now it seems to show up, even when I don't ask for it directly. I believe this same concept to be true of creativity. If we show up enough times and ask the universe to meet us there and deliver to us what we need, we will eventually receive it every time we show up—even if we don't ask for it directly, and even if it's not obvious to us right away.

Coming to the Practice

Writing is a practice. At the end of the day, it doesn't matter if the writing flows, or if we write ten pages or two sentences, or if what we write ends up in the trash. All that matters is that we came to the practice. Did we show up to the work? Did we give it our best attempt? Those are the questions we can be asking ourselves. It ultimately comes down to one thing: Are we doing the work we feel called to do? And if we are showing up to it regularly and giving it our best, then the answer is yes.

Motivating Ourselves to Take Action

I have a friend who loves to run, but some days he has a hard time motivating himself to run even a mile. When I asked him how he talks himself into it, he said that every morning when he wakes up, he says to himself, "Just put on your shoes, and go outside, that's all you have to do—if you don't want to run, you don't have to." He's clever and knows that, nine times out of ten, once he puts on his shoes and goes outside, he'll end up running.

I do the same with writing. I say to myself at times, "Just make a cup of tea, and sit down at the computer, that's all you have to do—if you don't want to write, you don't have to." Of course, I know that once I make my tea and sit down at the computer, I'll end up writing. The hardest part is sitting down at the computer in the first place when there are so many other things I could do.

The next time you have difficulty motivating yourself to write, try this approach. Make a cup of tea, and sit down at the computer or with a notebook, and if you want to stop after that, you can. Give yourself permission. But once you're there, you might be surprised to find that you want to keep going.

The Moment of Opportunity

There is a moment at the start of anything new or challenging when our first reaction is to pause and second-guess ourselves. I call this the "moment of opportunity." It's in these moments that we get to decide what our present reality will be, which inevitably paves the way for our future to follow.

I faced this decision each morning when I started waking up before work to take writing walks. As soon as my alarm went off at 6 a.m., I had to choose: either pull myself up out of bed, or go back to sleep and get another blissful hour of rest. These were my moments of opportunity. What's fascinating about these moments is that the feeling of discomfort they bring rarely lasts longer than a few seconds. The moment we say, "yes," and commit to taking action, our discomfort goes away and is replaced by feelings of peace and clarity. The moment I put on my shoes and grab my notebook and step out the front door, I know that's where I'm supposed to be.

The Time is Now

As artists we are continually getting better at our craft. The more we write or paint or sing or dance, the more we understand about it. As our level of intimacy with the work grows deeper, we learn what we were previously unaware of. We can look back at the work we have done and see that we are now more efficient, clear, concise, direct, and honest than we were when we started. We can see how much we have grown, but only upon examination of the past. What does this teach us? For one, it teaches us that we cannot be afraid to create imperfect work, because imperfect work is all there is. And second, it teaches us that we cannot wait until we are good enough or ready enough or talented enough, because that time may never come. The time to begin is *now*. Start on the path toward what you love today, in some small way. There's never been, nor will there ever be, a better time.

A Few Solid Minutes Each Day

It's easy to underestimate how much we can accomplish if we write for thirty minutes or an hour each day. I'm always astonished by what I accomplish over short increments of time. I wrote this entire book in my "off time," mornings and weekends spent slipping away into my own quiet corner of the universe to write a few sentences. A few solid minutes is all it takes. Just long enough to say, *I'm here. I'm listening. Is there anything you want to tell me?* The more often we pose this question to spirit, the more accustomed we become to hearing a reply.

A Daily Proclamation of Love

We are continuously choosing to be writers. We don't make the decision to be a writer once, and for the rest of our lives that's who we are. It doesn't work that way. We make the decision once and each day thereafter. We make the decision each time we show up to write, each time we set aside space for it, each time we put ourselves into the necessary mindset and give it priority over other things. It's similar to marriage in that we don't marry once and stay married for the rest of our lives without having to maintain that marriage every day. We marry and then we choose to remain married each day that follows through commitment, devotion, and sacrifice; through compassion that proves itself during the toughest times. Marriage is a *daily* proclamation of love, and writing is no different.

Conditioning Ourselves

I try to write every morning, even if only for a few minutes. Most mornings I fail miserably. I sleep in too late. I spend too much time showering and getting ready for the day. I make the mistake of checking the news or emails first thing when I wake up. But roughly half the time, I stay on track. I wake up in the morning and write for a few solid minutes before my busy day begins. I can tell you, I barely make a dent in the work most mornings, there's simply not enough time. But fortunately, that isn't why I do it. I do it because showing up consistently to the work strengthens my relationship with writing. Those few minutes, several mornings a week, remind me that I am a writer, a committed and devoted writer, who is taking the steps I want to take (albeit not perfectly, but to the best of my ability). Besides, when I have been writing consistently throughout the week, even if only for a few solid minutes here and there, I'm more likely to maintain that momentum in the days and weeks ahead.

Tipping the Scales

When I first started writing, it was only a small part of my life, something I did for a few hours each month. I didn't force myself to write more than I could, but I resolved to gradually start tipping the scales. Week by week, month by month, year by year, I put more time and energy into my writing practice. Not a lot more, just a little more, consistently. I worked full-time and wrote part-time on weekends, on my days off, in the mornings before work or in the evenings if I wasn't too tired. I learned that you don't have to be a full-time writer to take writing seriously. There are successful writers who have full-time careers, families to care for, mortgages to pay, friendships to maintain, and yet somehow they find a way to do it all. It might be that you're only able to write for a few hours each month, at first. That's okay. What matters isn't how much time you spend writing, it's that you're consistently moving closer to where you want to be. If you feel like writing part-time isn't enough, then gradually work toward tipping the scales. Week by week, month by month, year by year, put more time and energy into doing what you love.

The Writer's Path

The writer's path is different. There is not a clearly charted path the way there is for doctors or lawyers or teachers. In a way, it seems a solitary path because no two writers' paths are the same. There are no exams we take to see if we're ready to move on to the next level. No one is guiding us or telling us what to expect. We aren't graded or evaluated to know where we stand in relation to other writers.

For these reasons, being a writer requires us to be devoutly disciplined. Can you hold yourself responsible and show up consistently to the work? Can you persevere through fear and uncertainty? How strong is your vow to the writing life? We must take it upon ourselves to be stoic in our resolve. There are steps that we intrinsically know to take: write often, listen to your inner voice, approach life with a beginner's mindset, trust your intuition, write from your heart, and let the truth be your guiding force—both in your life and in your work.

The Merging of Dream and Reality

Becoming a writer happens in small stages, so small we often don't even realize it's happening. We start by writing a little at a time, and we continue writing a little at a time for the rest of our lives.

When you break down the big picture of "being a writer" into the smaller steps it takes to get there, it looks something like this: wake up, go about your day as you normally do, and somewhere in the midst of everything else that's taking place, sit down for a brief period of time and write. It continues like this each day for years, and while we're in the midst of doing it, we rarely see the gradual merging of our dream with reality. Little by little, we are becoming the person we want to be—making time to write, reading books by authors we admire, pulling our notebooks out to jot down ideas, getting up in the middle of the night when we feel inspired. These are the elements working together to bridge the gap between our dream and reality. These small demonstrations are powerful. And we only realize how powerful farther down the road, when we can look back and see how it all came together.

The Gradual Unfolding

It's not important to see the entire path before you take the first step. It's only important to see the first step. And even then, you don't need to see it with complete clarity. Close your eyes and feel your way into it slowly, inch by inch. A subtle gut feeling is enough—an instinct or a longing or a pull in one direction over another. As soon as the first step is taken you'll know more, and the instinct that led you there will transform into another instinct, a different instinct, an instinct you've never had before that will lead you to the next step... and the next... and so forth.

Look to nature and the elements around you, and you'll see that the universe unfolds gradually—the seasons of the year, the phases of the moon, the rising and falling of the tides, the orbits of the planets. Life is a gradual unfolding and each step illuminates the path ahead a little more, lighting the way just enough to reveal what comes next: the next word to write, or the next musical note to play, or the next corner of the canvas to paint. Trust the unfolding; it will lead you where you need to go.

Practice: Trusting the Feeling

Choose a theme that has special meaning to you. Perhaps nature or family or creativity—whatever you like. Write it down. Then, concentrating on your theme, close your eyes and listen for the first word that comes to you. If your theme is nature, that word might be willow tree or blossom or life. If your theme is family, it might be love or trust or even a person's name. Choose one word to start and write it down below your theme, and then follow it with as many other words as you can come up with that relate to your theme (or deviate from it—feel free to branch off in a different direction). With each word you write, feel for the word that most wants to be written. It doesn't matter whether it makes sense. Does it *feel* right? Does it resonate deep inside of you? This exercise is about trusting the feeling to lead you where you're meant to go.

Here's a list I recently wrote. My theme was *creativity* and my starting word was *intuition*.

Creativity
Intuition
Listening

Feeling
Trusting
Allowing
Giving
Receiving
Engaging
Sensing
Delving
Holding space
Silence
Honesty
Surrender
Holy
Grace
God
Unfolding

Go ahead and try it. See where it leads you. It may surprise you.

Why We Write

Art brings the subconscious to the surface.
It makes our thoughts and feelings known. It gives shape
and form to our ideas. It makes our beliefs visible.
Who am I? Why am I here? Where am I going?
These are questions art will answer.

Falling in Love with Books

When I was a child, my father used to take me to the public library a few miles away from our house. We would climb the towering steps to the main entrance, and he would lead me by the hand through the front door and past the rows of books organized alphabetically by last name, into the brightly lit room marked, "Books for Children." There he would leave me to myself for hours at a time. I would lose myself in the pages of fairy tales, mesmerized by the characters and their relationships to one another, and the challenges they faced, and the adventures they went on. When it came time to leave, he would find me on the floor, surrounded by stacks of books—*Berenstain Bears, Amelia Bedelia, Frog and Toad,* were some of my favorites. Those books were a precious commodity in our household; read nightly to me and my brother under the covers after we'd been tucked tightly into our beds, sending us off to sleep.

Do you remember when your love of reading began? What were your favorite books to read as a child? When did you first know you wanted to write?

Generations of Stories

I don't recall a time in my life without books or stories. Even before I learned how to spell, I was telling stories to my mother, who diligently typed them out word for word on the typewriter. Every night before bed, she read to me from our favorite books, and when we reached the end of a chapter she would say, "That's it! The end! Time for bed! Goodnight!" That was followed by fits of giggles and several more hours of reading until neither one of us could keep our eyes open any longer.

My father was the storyteller. He would make up elaborate adventure tales while my mother, brother, and I curled up under the covers around him. He would use the wall above our heads for sound effects: "Walk, walk, walk, walk, walk, walk, walk," he would say, emulating footsteps with his fingertips. Looking back on it now, I think this is the best way to teach a love so deep to someone else—love it so deeply for yourself first (as both my parents did).

Who Can Write?

Anyone who has an inkling of curiosity can write. That's all it takes. That and the willingness to explore it. I believe we all have it within ourselves to be writers if we want to, artists of any kind, but it does take practice. It does take a commitment. If we don't love writing deeply, and I do mean *deeply*, I doubt we will have what it takes to stick with it. If we do it because we think it will lead us somewhere, or to something, if the process alone is not enough to fulfill us, then I doubt we will stick with it. Anyone can be a writer, so long as curiosity and love are present. I would even go so far as to say the same is true of anything we want to devote our lives to and remain committed to—if curiosity and love are present, then I believe we have what it takes.

An Exploration into Awareness

The thing is, we are all artists, each one of us. We are creating art each day simply by being alive in the world and responding to it in our own unique ways. The physical act of writing is what makes us *conscious* of it. Are we aware of what we are creating? Are we aware of who we are choosing to be? Are we aware of how we are choosing to live our lives? Writing, more than anything else, is an exploration into awareness. No matter what we write—fiction, non-fiction, poetry, memoir, notes in a notebook that no one will ever see—writing makes us more conscious, and as we become more conscious, we become more mindful of how we live our lives.

Taking a Deeper Look

Each day there is something new to discover about ourselves and the world around us if we are willing to take a deeper look at it through art. Art brings the subconscious to the surface. It makes our thoughts and feelings known. It gives shape and form to our ideas. It makes our beliefs visible. Who am I? Why am I here? Where am I going? These are questions art will answer. There is an unearthing that takes place through the creative process, an unveiling of ourselves as we learn what we didn't already know. This is the key. *Art is about creating what is unknown to us.* We may paint a tree we've seen a thousand times or write about an experience from our childhood, drawing on what is familiar, but in the act of recreating it through writing or any other creative method, we are rediscovering what it means to us. Rediscovery takes place each time we show up to create, and there isn't a topic in the world—ourselves, our parents, the grass outside our window, our beloved dog, the toast we ate this morning for breakfast—that we can't write about or photograph or paint, and through the process, discover more than we know now.

Why We Choose to Be Writers

Naturally, if someone says she wants to be a tightrope walker, someone will ask, why? *Why do you want to be a tightrope walker when there are so many other easier professions you could choose?* I don't know which is easier, being a tightrope walker or being a writer.

Both require intense self-control, discipline, and practice. Both take years of hard work before you become any good. There's not a huge reward for either one, outside of your own personal satisfaction with the work you've done. But I suppose the reason why we choose to be writers (or tightrope walkers) is because we love it too much to choose anything else. No amount of comfort or security can compare to the joy we feel from writing.

The Deeper We Know Ourselves

Being a writer is really about falling in love with your deepening relationship to yourself. I have never met a writer who did not enjoy spending time alone, nor have I ever met a writer who did not enjoy the mysteries of their own mind. There is a great curiosity on the part of the writer that leads us to want to spend time alone with ourselves, and in this time we are getting to know ourselves, we are discovering who we are and what we believe, and we are surprising ourselves constantly. This is really what being a writer is all about. And the more time that we spend deepening our relationship with ourselves, the more sacred and meaningful this time becomes.

The Choice Writers Make

Writing is how we move through life, and it's how life moves through us. We could not experience life or share our experience of it as intimately as we do without writing. In that sense, we need it; we don't just choose it. It's ingrained in us, perhaps at an early age, perhaps even before we are born. But that isn't to say we have no choice at all. Just because we are born a certain way doesn't mean we will stay true to it or align our lives with it. *We have the choice to honor ourselves each day.* That's the choice we make: not only to be writers, but to remain true to who we are.

Writing Saves Lives

Writing has saved my life many times. One of those times came in my late twenties after a serious relationship came to a sudden end. I was depressed for months, barely eating, barely sleeping, unable to focus on work or anything else. I was miserable and my heart was broken, but somewhere deep inside I knew that all of the energy translating itself into my pain and suffering could be utilized. It could be redirected and channeled into other areas of my life that would help me grow and heal.

So I started to write, like a madwoman, because that was the state I was in (whatever I did, I was going to feel like a madwoman doing it—a madwoman cooking, a madwoman doing yoga, a madwoman chopping off all my hair). It was a great release. I wrote every day until I had no energy left in me, until I was physically exhausted from the emotional output. It felt exhilarating. Gradually, this process of channeling my pain in a creative way through writing led me back to health and happiness and hope again. Through that experience I learned how empowering writing can be; that even when we think we can't survive another day, there is a path to healing through writing.

Writing as a Coping Mechanism

Try not to let anything hold you back from writing. Too often, we let the problems and concerns we're dealing with become our excuse for not writing, forgetting that writing is one of the best coping mechanisms we have. If anything, we should write more during our times of discomfort. If we can write through them, it will help us to maintain a sense of centeredness and calm that stays with us through the chaos, like the eye of a storm. We will find nourishment and reprieve in our writing, especially during those times when we feel depleted in other areas of our lives.

The Midline

One of the greatest gifts that art offers us is that it brings us back to the midline. It reconnects us with our center, and when we are connected to that center we feel balanced, we feel grounded, we feel calm. With every word we write, with every brushstroke of paint upon the canvas, we bring ourselves closer to the midline, steering ourselves back to the center of ourselves, until we arrive and realize that *all is well*. This is the point we want our words and actions to come from. This is the point we want to live our lives from, make decisions from, fall in love from, speak our truth from, make love from, make art from. Whenever we feel ourselves veering off in a direction we don't want to go or losing control, we simply have to reach for what we love—writing, music, art—and it will pull us back. The more we practice this, hugging the midline so to speak, the easier it becomes to stay connected to it.

Giving Voice to Our Stories

There are some thoughts that will never leave us alone unless we write about them. They will follow us wherever we go, always trying to get our attention. Timing is important. We can't rush the process. Now might not be the right time to explore them. But more than likely the right time will come, and when it does we will have the opportunity to write about them. We will have the chance to listen to where those thoughts lead, and ask ourselves, *Why are they here? What do they want to teach us?*

The World as a Teacher

When we write about a topic, we are delving deeper into it, peeling back its layers, exploring what exists inside. We do that with some degree of curiosity, some degree of love for the thing we are writing about. We care to know what exists beyond what we already see. This is what makes writers unique; we want to know the truth, and we are willing to work for it. Writing is an unfolding, it opens the world up to us, like a flower, petal by petal, slowly revealing the center of the thing we are writing about— the real heart of it. This unfolding is how we make sense of the world we live in. It's how we learn from it. It's how we bear witness to its beauty. When I am writing and watching a story unfold, it becomes clear to me that the world is a beautiful place. It is teaching me every step of the way.

Practice: Redefining Words

I recently started a practice of redefining words. It's a playful practice, and I do it to help me tap into *the feeling* side of myself. I like to choose words that have special meaning to me. I tend to gravitate toward words like, "beauty," "clarity," "gratitude," "depth," "love," words that are somewhat abstract and leave something to the imagination. When we open ourselves up to the endless possibilities and tap into the feeling of each word—the feeling of beauty, the feeling of clarity, the feeling of gratitude—then we tap into something deeper within ourselves: who we are, what we have been through, the lessons we have learned. We can give new meaning to our words, based on our own experiences. This is powerful.

Here are a few of my attempts:

GENTLE – *the way my father tucked me into bed at night; my first dance, my first kiss, many other firsts; the lighting of a candle; prayer; leaves falling to the ground; the transition of seasons; waking up without an alarm; floating on my back in the ocean; being rocked to sleep in my mother's arms; holding my mother's hand as she slipped away.*

BEAUTY – *the universe and all its mysteries; waking up each morning to another day; the beach walks my father takes at sunrise; my parents on their wedding day; my grandmother with a scarf around her fragile shoulders; vulnerability; nature; the trust that's built after years of friendship; sharing a smile with a stranger; the first rays of morning light; authenticity.*

FRAGILE – *my mother in the days before she died; my front tooth which my brother knocked out accidentally with a tennis racket; the tiny wooden music box I had as a child (I called it "girl dancing"); my self-esteem in early adolescence; a newborn's tiny features, fingers, toes; my heart in the weeks following the break-up; my grandmother's jewelry inside a little box on my dresser; the human body; a human life; silence.*

Go ahead and try it. Write your own definitions for these words or any others you feel moved to write about. See where your imagination leads.

The Writing Practice

Being a writer isn't the result of anything we accomplish.
Being a writer is the result of one simple thing:
the consistent practice of writing.

Quietly Building a Writing Life

I think you have to be willing to spend years building a life as a writer before the world catches on. These years are critical because they're spent building a foundation—developing a writing practice, figuring out who you are as a writer, reading books that you love, creating a routine, getting to know yourself, learning your own creative rhythms and patterns. It's a time for exploring who you are, what you think, and how you feel. I believe this is the most important phase of becoming a writer. It's when we are bridging the gap between dream and reality. The dream of being a writer is wonderful, and so, too, is the reality of it, but what happens in between—the time when we are quietly building a writing life—is the most sacred part of all.

The Artist's Practice

The more often you practice stepping into the creative space, listening for the words, and opening yourself up to receive insight and inspiration from somewhere deep within you, the easier it will be to return to this space. It becomes easier each time, and each time we are teaching ourselves to step a little closer, listen a little deeper, and open ourselves up a little more. This is the artist's practice. You'll find that the more often you practice, the more eager the work will be to meet you in this space. It will wake you up in the middle of the night, it will greet you first thing in the morning, it will tug at the corners of your imagination throughout the day. That's the beautiful thing about the creative process: once you start to invoke it, it never goes away.

The Truth about Inspiration

I don't talk a lot about inspiration because I believe the word itself can be misleading. I believe we give it too much power over ourselves. More power than it deserves. If we are going to talk about inspiration, we have to start by dispelling some of the most common misconceptions:

- It is something we have to wait for.
- It exists outside of ourselves.
- It is difficult to tap into.
- It is elusive, hard to catch hold of.
- It is fleeting, it comes and goes on its own accord.
- It comes to some of us and not to others.

I don't believe any of the above are true, because all of the above render us powerless over inspiration, over our own creativity. We are not powerless. We are capable beyond our wildest imaginings, ready at a moment's notice, with unlimited potential as to what we can create. Inspiration is summoned the moment we step into our power, the moment our words meet the page, and it wants us to know:

- It is always available to us.

- It is something we bring forth from within ourselves.
- It is invoked through action.
- It is only as elusive as sitting down to write or picking up a paintbrush or snapping a photograph.
- It is everywhere, in all things, at all times.
- It is something everyone is capable of tapping into.

Developing the Practice

The practice is at the heart of writing. When we give all we can to our writing practice, it becomes a sacred practice, something we look forward to each day. Have you created a practice that fulfills you? Have you fallen in love with it? What is your relationship with your practice like? What does it mean to you? These are questions to ask yourself. The only thing you need to think about early on in your journey as a writer is giving yourself time to be alone with the work and creating the space for things to grow.

There is a relationship forming when we write, a relationship that takes us deeper into ourselves, into part of ourselves we haven't discovered yet. The practice of writing is spent exploring, narrowing in, listening to what is happening beneath the surface, training our cells to listen and respond. There are truths that are hidden there, perhaps even programmed into our DNA, our chakras, our energy lines. *Are we devoted to finding them?*

Do First, Understand Later

I went to a Waldorf School from kindergarten through sixth grade, and one of the principles that was instilled in us early on was *do first, understand later.* We were given the tools we needed to create and told to "explore," "experiment," "see where it leads you." We were handed beeswax and told to make something, before we ever knew what beeswax was, or why it smelled so good. We recited verses every morning written for us by our teacher, without knowing why it was important to stand with feet firmly planted on the ground and speak our voice. We were taught eurhythmy and moved through the room in our slippers, without knowing how the music soothed us, or why it felt so good to move our bodies. We were given paper and paints and told to use them, without knowing how to blend colors. We were given musical instruments and trusted to play them, even before we knew the notes.

There is something beautiful about doing first and understanding later. It is the way our lives are meant to flow. When we begin writing, it becomes clear what to write about. When we begin painting, we know what colors we feel most drawn to use. When we pick up an instrument, our fingers intuitively sense where to go. We can trust ourselves to take the first step, knowing that understanding will follow.

Art Relies on Intuition

Creativity is a series of small acts of faith performed one after another without any knowledge whatsoever of where they will lead. To draw a picture, we pick up a pencil and start moving it around on paper; we draw one small detail at a time without knowing what it will look like once all the details have been filled in. To write a book, we sit down at the computer and start typing; we put one word in front of the next without knowing what it will sound like when it's read from beginning to end. To capture a photograph, we pick up our camera and aim it at something beautiful; we sense when the moment is right to snap the picture without knowing how it will appear once we develop it. We rarely approach the work with a vision of what it will become; to do so would take us away from the spontaneity of the moment. *Art relies on intuition.* We are guided by that subtle, intuitive pull in one direction over another. Something within us moves us forward one small step at a time, and we never know where it's leading. One small act of faith after another in an unknown direction leads us to discover who we are and what we are capable of as artists.

The Path of Least Resistance

There is a myth that writing is only for lonely people who lock themselves away in their rooms and write from morning 'til night. While it may be true for some, most of the writers I know would disagree. There are many different paths to becoming a writer, an infinite number of ways, and the one that I suggest taking is the path of least resistance. Bruce Lee, the great martial artist, said, "Be like water making its way through cracks. Do not be assertive, but adjust to the object, and you shall find a way round or through it." He may have been talking about martial arts, but we can approach life and writing the same way, without insistence, without force, and we will be happier for it.

Go where you feel drawn. If you love to write in the mornings, then wake up early with a hot cup of tea and settle into that space. If you feel called to write children's stories, then give your heart to children's stories. If writing for three hours a month is enough to satisfy your craving, then make those three hours the best they can be.

Feeling at Home When We Write

What head space do you find yourself in most often?
   What heart space?
      How do you see the world each day?
         How do you feel when you wake up in the morning?
            What do you listen for?
               What do you look for?
                  What matters to you?

What matters to you is not the same as what matters to me. The ideas that you wake up with are not the same ideas that I wake up with. What you feel is different than what I feel. This is important. There is a unique distinction to the way each of us sees and thinks and feels. It's up to you to honor what makes you unique and write what you feel most comfortable writing. Some people feel at home in poetry. Some feel at home in fiction. Some in children's stories. Some in non-fiction. We can figure out what we're meant to write because we feel at home in its presence. As artists, we can speak in our natural way, think how we most love to think, feel how we most truly feel, and be absolutely completely ourselves just the way we are.

Exercising the Writing Muscle

Jane Yolen, who has written over 300 books (many of them for young children) shares this wise advice with aspiring writers: "Exercise the writing muscle every day, even if it is only a letter, notes, a title list, a character sketch, a journal entry. Writers are like dancers, like athletes. Without that exercise, the muscles seize up."

There are other things, too, that you can be doing to further your practice: read back over your work, edit it, brainstorm ideas and jot them down, hang out in bookstores for inspiration, reread your favorite books, plan who to thank in your acknowledgments, make a list of people you'll gift a copy of your book to when you finish it, contact them for their addresses, take your laptop to a coffee shop and practice tuning out the conversations around you, take a journal to the park and practice listening to the trees and the insects and the birds. All of this is action that is in line with writing because it helps you move closer to feeling like a writer. Explore it all. Exercise the writing muscle, the editing muscle, the reading muscle, the listening muscle, and so on, because all of it is helping you become a better writer.

A Path to Enlightenment

Tibetan monks spend days, sometimes weeks, constructing a single mandala or "sand painting," called a tson-kyil-khor. They begin drawing the geometric measurements and spiritual symbols into the mandala, and then they apply millions of grains of colored sand using tubes, funnels, and scrapers. Each mandala is said to represent the universe and the process of constructing it is considered a path to enlightenment—not the finished product, but *the process* of constructing it. Then, shortly after each mandala is created, it's destroyed, and a new one is begun, as a reminder of the temporary nature and impermanence of material life.

What if we approached our creative practice the same way, as if the process were what mattered most, not the end result? Would we make it easier on ourselves to show up each day? Would we take more risks? Would we be more inclined to try new things? Would we, too, become more enlightened and less attached to what we create?

The Principle of Repetition

The principle of repetition applies to any craft we hope to deepen our understanding of. In Ashtanga yoga, we practice the same series of postures each time, with little change or fluctuation. For years I have been following the same sequence of postures, and in each class I learn something new that I didn't know before. There is a deepening awareness of breath, alignment, focus, form in each practice. It is also true of writing. If we are willing to return to the practice, writing and rewriting, again and again, we will discover the deepest layers of ourselves through the work.

The artist is the variable in motion, and the work is the control. Whether we are rewriting the same paragraph, or singing the same song, or practicing the same yoga pose we have done a thousand times before, we will come away from it a more advanced practitioner when we realize there is more to learn.

The Impermanence of the Beginning

One reason why so many people have trouble getting started writing is because they approach the start with too much structure. They think they have to figure out every twist and turn in a story ahead of time. They think they have to know how a book will end before they can begin it, which couldn't be further from the truth. Nothing has to be known when we start writing, because by the time we reach the end, we will have rewritten the beginning countless times.

One of my favorite young adult authors, Roald Dahl, who wrote *Charlie and the Chocolate Factory, James and the Giant Peach,* and dozens of other stories, said of his experience: "By the time I am nearing the end of a story, the first part will have been reread and altered and corrected at least one hundred and fifty times." So, given the impermanence of every beginning, I believe it is best to think of the beginning as a launching pad, it simply sends us on our way. It launches us into the space of our imagination where our ideas can reach us, and that is where we need to be in order for the real work to begin.

Starting and Finishing

It's important to learn how it feels to start writing—to trust yourself to begin without knowing how you will finish and to commit to a direction without knowing where it will lead. This is essential, because for as long as we allow ourselves to feel scared of getting started, it will hold us back as writers. It's also important to become familiar with the feeling of ending what you have started. Lots of writers don't want to let go of their work. They become attached to it. It's never finished or good enough. Learn to draw your writing to a close. Learn to recognize when it's complete, even though there may be more you can do.

You can practice both, starting and finishing, by journaling in small increments each day. Pick up a pen and start writing about anything—the way the grass looks outside your window, what you dreamt about last night, what you're going to do today. Then, after you've said what you want to say, draw your writing to a close and mark it complete. Let it go. Move on to the next thing.

First Drafts

You've got to get it down the first time before anything else can follow. It doesn't matter whether it's good—first drafts usually aren't—what matters is that you get something down on the page. That's the hardest part and also the most essential, because the future of the work depends on that first step.

Here are some guidelines for first drafts:

- Approach your first draft gently and without expectations. Steer clear of perfectionism. What matters is that you say what you want to say. You can change it later.
- Be honest. Write as close to the truth of what you're feeling as possible. Honesty and authenticity are what the reader values most.
- Trust the writing to lead you where it wants to go. It will lead you into the unknown, but that's where all the best ideas are found.
- Build a relationship with your work. Be there for it. Listen to it. Make time for it. Stay committed to it. Speak highly of it. Believe in it.

• Embrace uncertainty. Not knowing what a book will become until the end is a gift, because in that unknowing, we find our faith in the process and in ourselves as writers.

The First Sentence

Start with a sentence. Any sentence. Take this sentence for instance. Or this one. Or this one. It isn't a perfect sentence. It isn't well thought out. It's just a sentence that is leading me to the next one. This one. That's all you have to do is write one sentence that leads to the next one. Don't worry about writing a "good" first sentence. Most likely, nobody will ever read the first sentence you write. Most likely, they'll read the great sentence you write on page five, which would never exist if it weren't for that terrible sentence you started with. Start anywhere and see where it leads you, but don't put off writing because you don't know where to begin. Begin with, "Well, this sucks, but I'm doing it anyway," or, "Okay, here we go, I'm writing my first sentence," or, "Ugh, I have no idea what to say, but here goes nothing." All of those are fine first sentences. All of those will lead you to your second sentence, and your third, and so on.

When I began writing my first book, I told myself, *don't worry about quality, simply think in terms of quantity.* Get stuff done. Make progress. Write anything. I knew that quality would come naturally with time and practice; my real challenge was getting started and showing up consistently to the work. I needed to write, regardless of what I was writing about, regardless of what anyone else thought, regardless of whether it was good or not. I needed words on the page. Period. I kept reminding myself, *quantity not quality*, which allowed me to worry less about what I was writing and concentrate more on getting something, anything, down on the page in front of me.

Making Decisions

Art is about making decisions. We commit. We lay down a word and then follow it with another word. We choose a color of paint and apply it to the canvas in front of us. We strike a chord and then strike another chord. Decisions made in a split second, without time to think or plan in advance; only time to feel. If the decision we make is wrong in retrospect, or if we change our mind later on, that's okay. What matters is that the decision we make now leads us to the next decision, which leads us to the next decision. What matters is that we are making progress. At any time, we can change the decisions we have made in the past. We can cross out our words, or paint over what we have painted before, or change the lyrics of a song. Creativity is an ongoing process. It doesn't end, and each decision we make is only a starting point. We are constantly building upon what has come before.

Leaving Ourselves Freedom

What would I say if I could say anything today? What feels important? That's a question I sometimes ask myself at the start of a writing session. Then, without trying to direct it, I write in whichever direction it leads me. The wild and exciting thing is that each day the answer is different; each day this question leads me somewhere new, somewhere I wasn't expecting. That's the beauty of writing. Each day is a new beginning with new possibilities. For this reason, it's important to keep our ideas general. If our ideas are too specific, if we know our entire plot from beginning to end before we even start, we leave ourselves little freedom to write from where we are. If we say we want to write a story about a black cat who befriends an elephant, and on Monday they eat berries, and on Tuesday they swim in the river, and on Wednesday they play in the park, and on Thursday they have a picnic, and on Friday they catch fish, and on the weekend they sleep in late... then we're not leaving ourselves a whole lot of freedom to explore. But if we say we want to write a story about a black cat who befriends an elephant, and together they set off on great adventures... then we're leaving ourselves freedom to see where the story wants to lead us. Where we are on any given day is changing, and we have to give our stories permission to change with us.

Taking a Light-Hearted Approach

When it comes to being creative, it's entirely up to you to do it the way you want to do it, when you want to do it, how you want to do it, where you want to do it, for how long you want to do it. If there is one thing that's important to realize about the creative process, it's that there is no right or wrong way to do it. There is nothing you have to do, nothing you have to be, and nothing you have to prove. Take a deep breath and remind yourself that there are no shoulds. There are no musts. There are no rules. There is limitless possibility. There is freedom. There is room to experiment and explore. Create when you are ready, as often or as infrequently as you like. And if the thought of writing a poem or painting a picture is weighing heavily upon you, then remind yourself that the purpose of art isn't to burden us; the purpose of art is to liberate us. Take a light-hearted approach. Create because it feels good, because it's fun, because you have everything to gain and nothing to lose.

Releasing Control

Picture a feather in the wind. A feather is not responsible for making the wind blow. It is not responsible for knowing where the wind will take it. It has no control over whether it will be blown to the east or the west, the north or the south. A feather is only responsible for being a feather and doing what feathers do. *And so are we only responsible for being who we are and doing what we know how to do.* We cannot force the winds of inspiration to blow. We cannot force the magic to work on our behalf. We cannot force the arrival of new ideas. We can only do what we have the power to do: Show up. Be present. Listen. Observe. Write. Then we must release control of everything else and trust that the winds of inspiration will blow, because that is what winds are made to do. We don't have to force anything. Inspiration will come at the right time. Magic will come at the right time. New ideas will come at the right time. And we will be there to receive it, simply by doing what's in our power.

What to Write About

Never ask yourself, what should I write about? Or, what would other people want to read? This takes us away from what we are individually capable of. It ignores passion and injects uncertainty. Ask yourself, instead, what am I dying to write about? What would I hate to leave this world without being able to say?

A Life of Its Own

I can never say for sure how long it's going to take me to write a book, because I don't know what a book wants to become until I see it take form in front of me. The moment I start to write, the work develops a life of its own. It becomes a living, breathing, conscious entity, and I become its caregiver, guiding it along. To say that a book will be finished in one year or five years is nearly impossible. I don't have that much control over it. It's not up to me, alone. I have to respect the work and allow it the freedom it needs to become what it wants to be. I usually have a vague idea of how much time it will take to reach its full potential, but I can never say for sure with any amount of certainty. I have to rely on the work to tell me what it needs, and I know that the work is trusting me to listen.

Staying with the Work

For every one thing I write that I am able to finish—as in send to my editor, publish, and make peace with letting go of—there are probably one hundred things that are left unfinished. Half-written poems, books that never found their way, ideas that sparked and fizzled out too soon. I'm rarely able to return to something I wrote in the past and finish it. Where I am now is different from where I was then. I'm not the same person. I don't have the same ideas.

I've learned that the best way to finish something I start is to never leave it. I must be consistently working on it until the end. That doesn't mean there aren't ebbs and flows or breaks in the work; I just try never to leave it for long—not more than a few weeks or months at most. I know how hard it is to return once I have grown apart from it. I have to return while I'm still the same person I was when I wrote it. I have to be in relatively the same place in my life, with the same questions and challenges. I've learned that you have to stay with your work. Wherever you go, take the work with you. Keep it close to you at all times.

The Many Moods of Writing

Whatever you're feeling right now, bring it into your writing. Give it a direction. Allow it to serve a purpose. Don't let that emotion go to waste. Write under every emotional context you can stand to write under, because that's how you'll grow and evolve as a writer. That's how you'll learn what you're capable of. You wouldn't want to only write when you're feeling happy, nor would you want to only write about one character for the rest of your life. To grow and evolve as a writer, you want to experience the entire spectrum of your emotions under the spotlight of the page. How does anger translate to the page? How does grief? How does fear, confusion, sadness, joy?

Some emotions that we wouldn't think to be conducive to writing can lead us to create our best work. Impatience can be a powerful tool for getting down to the most fundamental layers of the work. If the work isn't good enough, impatience cuts right through it. Exhaustion is similar because it forces us to approach the work with less attachment. If a sentence doesn't work, it's gone, move on. Anger can be good if it invokes us to write from a deeper emotional state than we're used to writing from. Same with grief. Stress can make us more determined to get the work done because we have a limited time and capacity to do it; we have no choice but to push through it. Every emotion lends itself to writing and has the potential to take our writing deeper if we have the courage to explore it.

Give Everything to the Page

Give yourself to the page when you write. Give everything. Give your joys and your sorrows. Give your fears and your failures. Give your suffering and your sickness and your pain. Give your imperfections. Give your vulnerabilities. Give your hopes and your dreams and your aspirations. Give every last breath. Give and give and give of yourself until there is nothing left to give, because only then will you discover that there is always more you can give; even when you think you have reached the end, there is always farther you can go. Your readers will feel what you have given, and the more you give, the more they stand to receive. Give of yourself like there is no tomorrow; like now is all there is.

Talking about Our Work

There is something sacred about holding our work (our creative vision) close to our hearts and saving the casual conversation of it for later, once we have done all that we can do. Just as there is something sacred about wishing when we blow out the candles on a birthday cake or praying late at night when we're all alone. Silent observance is a powerful thing. When we choose to hold our work in silence, as if it were a wish or a prayer, our energy stays with us—it remains intact, sacred, whole. But when we choose to talk about our work, I have found that oftentimes our energy leaves us—it gets channeled into criticism or complaints; it manifests as fear or self-doubt. I invite you to observe this in action for yourself. See what happens when you hold your work close to your heart and speak of it very little. How does it feel? How does your relationship with the work evolve? Then see how it feels to talk of it openly, without restriction. What is gained? What is lost?

Where We Carry Emotions

Yoga teaches us that our pain from traumatic experiences is carried in the energy centers of the body. We might carry the death of our mother in our solar plexus, our brother's depression in our root chakra, our fear of drowning in our limbic system. The body remembers and holds onto everything that's ever happened to us like a safe.

When we write, we can't skim the surface or relive the experience solely from our mind's memory; we have to go deep into the energy centers of the body, where the actual *feeling* of the memory is stored. The body remembers the slow surrender when we said good-bye to our mother for the final time. The body remembers the frustration of words that went unheard to a brother in pain. The body remembers how terrified we were when we nearly drowned as a child and feared that no one was coming to save us. The body remembers our pleading, our praying, our crying; it remembers our laughter, our love, our joy. The body remembers everything, even the things our mind forgets. When we write, we subconsciously travel deep into the energy centers of the body to recall the truths of those experiences and emotions.

Aligning with the Truth

The writer's life is devoted to aligning with the truth, and that's a beautiful thing to devote one's life to. It's not easy to be in direct alignment with the truth though. Language alone takes us off by a few degrees, because the words we use to express ourselves can never express the total depth or complexity of our feelings. So, being a writer is about aligning with the truth *to the best of our ability*, both in our lives and on the page. It's like lining up an arrow to shoot. The path the arrow takes when it leaves our fingertips depends entirely upon the alignment of our body before we let go. If our body is erect, if our arms are outstretched, if our index finger is pointed, if our eyes are focused exactly where we want the arrow to go, then we will hit our target. In the same way, if we are aligning our lives with the truth—thinking and speaking and acting with integrity—then the moment the words leave our fingertips for the page, it will become apparent that we shot straight.

The Rhythm of Language

A story isn't only told through words, as we know so well from music. Music can make us feel happy or sad, calm or excited, sensual or nostalgic. That's the power of rhythm. It bypasses our intellect and goes straight to our emotions. It's quite intuitive that way. When we write, the rhythm of our words serves as an undercurrent to the story, guiding the reader's emotions. A mystery novel might follow a choppier rhythm to create a sense of anticipation and suspense in the reader. A nursery rhyme might follow a slower and softer rhythm to put the child to sleep, or it might be more upbeat if it aims to be silly and playful.

If we listen closely we find that rhythm is everywhere, in everything. It's in the sound of our footsteps upon the earth, the steady pulse of our heartbeat, the gentle inhale and exhale of our breathing, the heavy downpour of a late afternoon thunderstorm, the hum of crickets through the grass at night, even in silence there is rhythm. It makes you wonder if perhaps these are the undercurrents to an even greater story that is being told right now, somewhere far, far away.

The Imaginations of Children

Play, for a child, means dreaming infinite possibilities into reality—turning a sofa into a sailboat and drifting off into the sea; making sheets and pillows into an impenetrable fortress; planting seeds with the certainty they'll grow into giant beanstalks. To a child, anything is possible. There are no limits. If they can imagine it, they can experience it.

Some people think that writing for children is easier than writing for adults, but the question we should be asking ourselves is, *can we write to their level?* Can we tap into their level of creativity? Their level of imagination? Their level of spirituality? Are we as good at playing make-believe as children are? Are we as curious and as free? Writing for children challenges us to tap back into the feelings we once felt as children, so that we can remember what it's like to sail across an open sea in our pajamas, or camp out in a fortress made of sheets, or become something we've never been before—a ballerina, a princess, a superhero. It challenges us to remember how limitless we have always been and always will be.

The Parts of a Book

I once made a game of examining the parts of a book each time I went into a bookstore. One time I went in and decided I was going to study titles. Which titles drew my attention? Why? What made a title great or not so great? The next time I decided to study covers. Which covers attracted me? Which colors caught my eye? What makes a cover beautiful? Another time, I studied tables of contents. How did the chapters flow together? What order did they follow? Did they do a good job of summarizing what each section was about? Another time, I looked only at first sentences of first chapters. What made for a strong first sentence? What did it tell the reader about the rest of the book? Did it make me want to read on further?

There are so many parts of a book that we can examine in this way: layout, acknowledgments, dedications, endorsements, illustrations, author biographies, subtitles, last sentences of last chapters. By seeing what other authors have done and learning what we respond to, it gives us a vision for our own books to follow.

Creating Order

There are times when writing is like cleaning a house. When we clean a house, there is a period of disarray that comes first before there is order. During that time, we have to upend everything before we can put it back together. On the surface, things appear worse than when we started—clothes are strewn across the floor, dishes are piled high in the sink, everything is pulled out of its place—but in reality, the chaos is all part of creating order. It isn't until the final moments, when everything is put back where it belongs, that we see the order we've been creating all along. Try to remember this when you are writing, and especially when you are editing. There are times when we go back over our work and upend everything—rewrite the same paragraph thirty times, take it apart, cross it out, move it around, pick it apart, throw it away, start over again. On the surface, it seems like we are going nowhere, like there is chaos at every turn, but in reality we are on our way to creating order. The fact that we are in an upheaval to begin with means that we are further along than we realize. We have turned the work upside down and on its head, which is half the challenge in itself; now the fun is putting it back together.

Choosing a Title

A title is a funny thing. We have a limited amount of space, a few words at most, to share a valuable message with the reader. And yet, we have great freedom when it comes to choosing a title. The challenge of saying what we need to say in such a small space requires us to expand our thinking in new ways. *How can I fit something so large into a space so small?* Fortunately, we don't have to shrink the universe to make it fit into the lens of a telescope, we simply have to point our telescope toward the stars. The same is true of choosing a title. We don't have to fit the entire book into the title, we just have to choose a title that serves as a lens, inviting the reader to look deeper.

Here are some qualities of strong titles:

- It paints a clear picture of what's inside the book.
- It tells the reader what they're going to learn.
- It clarifies the purpose or intention of the book.
- It asks a question the book answers or it answers a question the book asks.
- It invokes a reaction in the reader, such as surprise or intrigue or hope or fear.

- It invites the reader to learn something they don't already know or want to better understand.
- And, most of all, it awakens the reader's curiosity.

Committing to a Title

I like to give a title time to grow with me—months, sometimes years—before I commit to it and say for sure, *YES, you are the one.* I like to move in with it first, get to know it on a deeper level, drink my tea with it in the morning, fall asleep with it each night, and even fight with it on occasion. And if I'm still in love with it after living together for some time, then I know I'm ready to commit. It's not an easy commitment to make. I'm going to spend the rest of my life with a title, so for that reason I'm not looking for titles that I like a lot or fall instantly in love with. I'm looking for titles that withstand time. I'm looking for titles that will mean more to me 30 years from now than they mean to me today.

The Distance between Us and Them

A new exercise I recently experimented with was writing down another author's work as if it were my own. I took the work of one of my favorite authors, Madeleine L'Engle, and I wrote out several paragraphs from her book, *Herself: Reflections on a Writing Life.* I typed them into the same document as my own manuscript on writing, so that I could read my words and her words side by side.

I was surprised to realize that another author's work appears less intimidating when it's lifted from the pages where it belongs and observed in a different context. Through the process of writing her words, I recognized similarities and differences in our writing styles. I noticed details of style and voice that I hadn't noticed in earlier readings of her work. Sometimes as simple as a tendency to write "it is" more often than "it's," or to begin a new sentence with a conjunction. The most valuable lesson this taught me is that there is less separating us from the authors we admire than we once thought.

A Question of Profession

I have always admired writers who are able to say with confidence, "I am a writer," when asked what they do for a living. They say it so matter-of-fact, without hesitation, as if their entire lives haven't been spent coming to terms with it (as mine undoubtedly has). I've always wondered how they do that. At what point does it become official? When do we earn the right to call ourselves writers? When we publish our first book? When we publish our second or third book? When we are able to financially support ourselves through writing? After years of asking myself these questions, I now believe that being a writer isn't the result of anything we accomplish. Being a writer is the result of one simple thing: *the consistent practice of writing.* In the words of Annie Dillard: "How we spend our days is, of course, how we spend our lives." If you spend your days writing, then you are a writer, and you have every right to say with confidence, "I am a writer," when asked what you do for a living.

The Sacred Scrap Pile

During a lecture I attended several years ago to hear the poet Chase Twichell speak, she told the audience that she keeps two scrap piles. The first one she calls "the orphanage," where she keeps the single lines she loves and hopes to find a home for one day. The second one she calls "the compost," where she keeps all the scraps and pieces of writing that might be worth returning to at some point.

A scrap pile is a simple document where you keep all the writing you've done that isn't serving you at the moment. We do so much writing over the course of our lives, and where are we supposed to put it all? It isn't all going to be writing we love, or writing we want to publish, or writing that we have an immediate use for. But that isn't to say that one day it won't serve a purpose. Whenever something isn't working, or I'm not wild about it, or I can't figure out what to do with it… into the scrap pile it goes! And I'm on to the next thing. What a joy it is to move something I've been working on for so long into that scrap pile and forget about it, for the moment anyway.

Honoring the Message

There is a message in what we write, and the message is the most important thing to bring through in our work. Anything we hope to pass on to the reader is secondary to the message, because if the message lacks clarity it will have little emotional effect on the reader. It starts with clearly delivering the message first, and when we are able to do that, then we can have any effect on the reader we wish to have, so long as they are open to it. We can inspire them, encourage them, offer them a path to hope and healing, show them a new way of seeing the world. This is rarely achieved on the first attempt though. It takes many drafts to tune the writing so that the message comes through clearly. This is the role that rewriting plays in our work. It's like wiping away the fog on a window—every time we rewrite our work, we wipe away a little more, until eventually we are able to see the message shining through, bright and clear. It's in the rewriting that we have the ability to honor our message the way it deserves.

Becoming Honest

Think of editing as an opportunity to make your work more honest. That's the purpose of editing—to refine what you have written by adding layers of depth or perhaps lifting layers that weighed down what you were saying, overcomplicating it. *Clear, simple, and true.* That's a good motto when it comes to writing. How can you deliver your message in the clearest, simplest, truest way? As you read back over your work, look for ways to make your message more honest, and in that process you'll find that you are becoming more honest with yourself.

A Stranger to the Work

When we return to our work after spending some time away from it, we see it again with fresh eyes. We read it again with a fresh perspective, as if we are reading it for the first time. This is critical. We can't judge our work while we are creating it, because we are too immersed; we are too deep in its layers to see it from the outside. Give yourself at least a week, or a month, before you return to it. Can you read it back to yourself and be surprised by what it's saying? That's the true test. That's when you'll know you're ready to edit it. If the words are still so fresh in your memory that you remember what's coming next, then not enough time has passed. But if you sit down in front of it and think to yourself, *wow, did I write this?!* then you can be a stranger to the work and read it objectively.

Making Peace with Imperfection

Perfectionism has no place in writing. If it makes you feel bad, if it holds you back, if it slows you down, if it impedes your growth, if it prevents you from moving forward, it has no place in writing. By all means rewrite your work as many times as it takes to say what you really mean. Tell the truth clear. Say all that's necessary, and say only what's necessary. But understand that even after you've rewritten your work many times, there will still be more that can be done. There will always be room for improvement.

Making peace with imperfection is part of every artist's journey. There comes a point when you have to be willing to say, *enough... I've done my best... I've given it my all... it's time to move on to other books or other paintings or other songs.* If you hold onto your work and keep perfecting it to no end, your work is serving no one. But if you can embrace the beauty and the wholeness of your work in spite of its imperfections, then your work can serve the world. *Allow your gifts to be seen, as well as your flaws.*

The Makings of a Miracle

When a book comes together, it is a miracle. It is nearly impossible to fathom how a series of small steps taken over a long period of time can eventually lead us to cross the same finish line that has been crossed by every great writer and artist who has come before us. It is nearly impossible to see that we are walking in their footsteps, traveling the same path they have traveled, when we are traveling so slowly and taking such soft steps—a few hours writing on weekends, a few paragraphs in the evenings after work, thoughts journaled in a notebook throughout the day.

It isn't until we reach the end and cross over the finish line that we can see the stunning perfection of the path we have traveled upon. It is a miracle that we are able to reach our final destination *one step* at a time. It is a miracle that we are able to write a book *one word* at a time. It is a miracle that we are able to live a full and meaningful life *one day* at a time. When we observe what makes a miracle a miracle, we are able to see what exists at the center of it. Love. Intention. Faith. Commitment. Courage.

Final Drafts

There is no formula that will tell you when a book is finished. There are only questions you can ask yourself. Are you satisfied with it? Have you done all that you can do? Is it as close to the truth as you can write it? Are you ready to move on from it? You can also ask the work directly if there is more it needs from you. Sometimes, before I go to bed at night, I will ask the work to show me what it needs in my sleep. Or you can write it in the form of a question on paper and see if an answer comes to you. Final drafts are just as mysterious as first drafts. You won't know what it feels like to finish until you cross over that line, and it's different for every writer.

Here are some guidelines for final drafts:

- Rewrite what you have written until you can read it back to yourself and love every word.
- Listen to the work. Ask it to tell you what it needs. It will tell you when it has more to say and it will tell you when it is finished.
- When you think you are done, take a break from it for a while. Then return to it and see if you still love it as much as before.

- Resolve to love it no matter what. Whether you publish it or not. Whether other people read it or not. Whether it's the best book you are capable of writing or not. If you have grown through the process of writing it, it is worthy of your love.

Nearing the End

When we near the end of a book, we sometimes feel overcome with fear because we are so close to a place we have been working to reach for so long. It's not uncommon to turn our back on the work, to suddenly feel like we're too busy to finish what we started, to question whether it's good enough or if we should start over again from the beginning. This feeling of fear has come over me many times as I'm nearing the end of a book. I want to give up; I lose hope; I feel so close and yet so impossibly far away.

This feeling of nearing the end is similar to how we feel when we are nearing the beginning. We are overcome with fear of the unknown; we feel overwhelmed with the magnitude of what lays before us; we question ourselves and what we are capable of. *Do I really have what it takes to do this?* When we are nearing the end, we must remember all that we learned in the beginning, because the same lessons apply. Do you remember how difficult it was? Do you remember how impossible it felt? What did you do then to push off from the edge in spite of your fears?

Stepping Away and Stepping Back

There are times, after a book is finished, when I'll think to myself, okay, now it's time for a break. I'll take a few months off from writing to sleep in, or read my favorite books, or wander around the house looking for something to catch my interest. But it doesn't take long to realize that something is missing from my life, before I start to think, what am I doing? What exactly am I "breaking" from? Are these days of aimless wandering really better than the joy I feel from listening to the world speak? Better than the surprises that greet me each morning when I sit down at my desk with no idea of what to write and begin writing? Better than communing with the spirit of every leaf or stone or bird or tree? Is this what I am breaking from? Is this what I sacrifice by stepping away from the work? *I must return to it quickly, before I forget it and lose it entirely!*

Practice: Rewriting the Work

Once you've written something, *anything*, try rewriting it. It's in the rewriting that we are able to tweak and finesse the words just so to say what we really mean. Here's how to do it: Have the original work you wrote in front of you. Then, read your work back to yourself and simultaneously rewrite or retype it, word for word, feeling for the truth and accuracy of each word you write. *The key is to write what you've already written, as if you are writing it for the first time, using what you've already written as a map or a guide.* Think of it like tracing over the work you've done, with more precision and care each time. This allows you to feel the essence of each word; to feel whether each word achieves its full potential on the page. Write slowly, listen to the words closely, and feel them with all your senses. It's not an intellectual knowing, it's a physical knowing. When a word is right, we feel it with our entire being. This process of rewriting our work allows us to feel everything we felt the first time we wrote it, all over again. Sometimes we still resonate with it and the same truth applies to where we are now in our lives. Other times we feel the truth even deeper than we felt it the first time, and we are able to add layers of depth and clarity.

The Struggles
of Writing

Fall in love with all of it: the good and the bad,
the times when everything is working
and the times when everything is not,
the inspired moments and the blocked moments alike.
Because all of it is adding to us—making us
better writers and better human beings.

The Burden of a Dream

There are two ways of looking at a dream. There are some people who look at a dream, and they think about what that dream must amount to. It must amount to success. It must amount to money. It must amount to making a difference in the world. It must amount to becoming famous in that industry. It must amount to recognition and respect. For these people, the dream quickly becomes a burden, and they move through life carrying around this burden and feeling miserable because the weight is so great.

Then there are people who look at a dream, and they see it for what it already is, without anything else attached. It is what they love to do. It is what brings them happiness and peace. It is a source of growth. It is a source of comfort. It is who they are and who they came to this world to be. For these people, the dream carries no weight at all. They are able to step easily into the path of their dream feeling light, feeling happy, feeling blessed, feeling free, because there is no burden they have to carry.

Tell me, how are you looking at your dream?

What to Embrace and Release

The only way that I have been able to create a life as a writer has been by embracing what is and releasing what isn't. There have been times when I stopped writing completely. I embraced it. I released my fears that maybe I would never write again. There have been times when I wrote all the time, nearly every day. That, too, I embraced. I released my worries that maybe I wasn't making enough time for my family, or I was letting my life pass me by as I sat alone at my desk each day. There have been times when all I could do was show up a few times a month, and even then it was with trepidation and fear. I embraced it. I released the thoughts that it wasn't enough; I should be doing more. Our lives will always be changing. Our routines will always be changing. So the wisest thing we can do is embrace what is while releasing what isn't. The sooner we can do that, the sooner we can enter into the flow of *what is*, and be fully present and at peace where we are.

The Creative Monster

What is it about sitting down to create that can seem so scary? I encourage you to think about it. We all have beliefs about the creative process and our ability (or inability) to invoke it that stand in our way. Many of us make the creative process out to be some sort of monster: a large, looming shadow that follows us wherever we go. We think we have to carve out hours of time each day to satisfy its insatiable hunger. We think we have to sacrifice everything—our children, our career, our relationships—to this monster, this beast of a thing called *creativity*, which demands all of us. It's no wonder we're so scared.

But what if we approached the work as if it were secondary? A side-project sort of thing? Something we do here and there for a few minutes at a time—five minutes in the morning, twenty minutes on the weekend, an hour when no one else is around—with the mindset that it needn't take us away from anything else? Would it be any easier? Would the monster we fear seem any less intimidating? *The trick is to make it as easy on ourselves as possible, so we realize that creativity isn't as scary as it seems.*

The Presence of Fear

There is no rule that says we have to keep fear separate from our work. There is no rule that says art is for the fearless only. We know that isn't true. Georgia O'Keeffe said it best when she said, "I've been absolutely terrified every moment of my life—and I've never let it keep me from doing a single thing I wanted to do." Her paintings would not be what they are today if she hadn't experienced fear and painted anyway. She didn't try to deny fear or avoid it; she acknowledged it, and then worked alongside it to create the work she came here to do. *And so can you.*

What If We Never Try?

"There are so many great authors in the world, and I'll never be as good as them, so what's the point in even trying?" This is a common response I hear from people who want to write but are scared. When I hear this it leads me to wonder, what if Plato had never had the courage to follow in the footsteps of his teacher, Socrates? And what if Aristotle had felt too inadequate to follow in the footsteps of Plato? What if Anne Morrow Lindbergh (one of my favorite authors) had never written *Gift from the Sea*, which appeared on the *New York Times* bestseller list for 80 weeks, because other female authors were already writing about women's lives in the mid-20th century? And what if Anne's daughter, Reeve Lindbergh, had never written and published over 25 books, because her mother was already a bestselling author beloved by millions of people? What if I had never written this book, because thousands of other books about writing already exist? And what if you never write what is inside of you?

I don't believe that the number of great books written, or theories proven, or scientific discoveries made should ever prevent us from searching deeper and exploring further in our own lives. There will always be more to create and more to explore and more to discover. The purpose of art is to keep us expanding. So it is our responsibility to expand upon what has come before us, and it will be the responsibility of future generations to expand upon what we do, right now, in our time on Earth.

The Unconquerable Mountain

There is a sense within all writers that we're not good enough, we're not ready, we have so much standing in our way. Being a writer is seen as an unconquerable mountain we are not nearly equipped to climb. The writers who came before us... *they* were equipped for the journey. They had better tools, better skills, more experience. They knew what they were doing. That's what we tell ourselves anyway, but the truth is that writing is not an easy path for anyone. No one is prepared to make the journey. Writing takes all of us, even the best writers (*especially* the best writers) into uncharted territory. It's supposed to be overwhelming. It's supposed to be terrifying and exciting. We're going where we've never gone before. We don't know what we're going to find, but we set off anyway in search of new ideas, new ways of thinking, new ways of existing in the world.

Accepting Fear and Uncertainty

I think we have to accept the presence of fear, and even go so far as to make peace with it, if we wish to become what we are capable of as artists. If we are unwilling to face the darkest side of ourselves, how will we ever discover what lies beyond the darkness? If we are unwilling to face what scares us or makes us uncomfortable, how will we ever discover that fear and discomfort are gifts that lead to greater clarity? When we can accept what scares us—that we don't know where we're going or how to get there, that the road that leads us there might be long and winding and mostly uphill, that there's a chance we might not make it all the way to the top—then it becomes easier to move with our dreams, because we are inviting fear to join us in the journey. When we can accept fear, we no longer have to fight against it. We free ourselves, knowing that fear is no longer standing in our way; it's coming along for the ride, and a great ride it will be.

Lighting Fire to Our Wants

If you want to be an artist, I suggest you stop *wanting* to be an artist and start writing, painting, playing, composing, creating. Throw your wanting out the window. Hold a ceremony for it if you like. Write down your wants on a piece of paper, and light fire to them… watch them disintegrate before your eyes. Cut them up into tiny pieces of paper and toss them into the wind… watch them float away. Buy a shovel and bury them… write them a eulogy, and say your final good-byes. After that, don't ever speak of them again. Speak instead about the work you are doing, the progress you have made, the lessons you are learning, the growth that's taking place. Ask yourself at the end of each day, each week, each month: *Have I done the work I wanted to do?* That's all that matters. You'll see.

The Stories We Tell

Talking about writing can be a tricky thing. When we talk about something aloud, we start to tell a story about it, and the story we tell soon becomes our truth—or what we *believe* is our truth. This is powerful. If we tell the wrong story, we will begin to believe that writing is hard, we're not good enough, there's not enough time for it, it's lonely and isolating, we're uninspired, we're overwhelmed, and countless other disempowering beliefs that hold us back. The stories we tell about writing should uplift us and empower us, encourage us and move us forward. Talk about writing in the way you *want* to be talking about writing. If you want to be writing more, say that you're finding moments throughout your days to slip away and write for a few minutes. If you want to feel more confident in yourself as a writer, say that you're beginning to trust yourself and follow your instincts more than ever before. If you want to stop letting fear hold you back, say that you're learning to accept the presence of fear and create alongside it. Say these things now—to yourself and others—and soon you will start to see their truth.

Working with Limiting Beliefs

I'm not inspired. I'm not ready. I don't know where to start. I'm not a creative person. These are beliefs we may not consciously be aware that we have, yet they subconsciously cause us to put less important things first before our writing practice—things like organizing our underwear drawer, cleaning out the garbage disposal, hitting refresh on our emails, watching TV shows we don't even like. When we avoid the creative practice in lieu of less important things, it may be our subconscious telling us that we have limiting beliefs that are rooted in fear. The solution isn't to try to overcome our limiting beliefs, and then turn our attention to writing. The solution is to turn our attention to writing and then, over time, those limiting beliefs will fall away. When we are in the flow of writing, our subconscious observes that we are in motion, taking action, listening to our intuition, aligning with our higher self, putting our faith in something greater. And when we are doing these things, we develop new, empowering beliefs that begin working on our behalf to bring us closer to our dreams.

Limiting Belief #1: I'm Not Inspired

This limiting belief stems from the idea that inspiration is separate from us and we have no control over it. Let us dispel this myth right now, because there is no truth to it. *Inspiration must be invoked. It must be prompted, invited, encouraged, egged on, poked, prodded, and nudged.* How? By showing up to the work and getting started. When we sit down to the work and begin, we are showing inspiration that we are ready, but we must be willing to go first. We must take the first step, and not just once, but every time. Then we will see that inspiration is *always* ready to respond. It is always ready to meet us. It never has sick days. It's never too tired. It's never too busy. It has no other priorities. It is solely devoted to our work. If it were up to inspiration, we would work all the time. But it isn't up to inspiration—it's up to us. We get to decide when it's time to work. Inspiration is patient, it will wait for us as long as we ask it to, but it wants to be engaged. It exists for a reason, and its purpose is to help us create. *We are co-creators with inspiration.* Just as we need it, it needs us; and the more often we call on it, the more often it will be there for us.

Limiting Belief #2: I'm Not Ready

Are we ever truly ready? Or is readiness an illusion, an imaginary state? Perhaps we think to ourselves, *I'll know when I'm ready because I'll feel inspired and excited and eager to begin...* but then we find ourselves thinking the same thoughts months or years later and wondering when it will happen. Perhaps we think, *when it feels easy, then I'll know I'm ready...* but for as long as we are stepping into the creative process, with all its unknowns, we will never feel entirely at ease. We have to take small steps in the direction we want to go—show up to write each day, scribble in our notebooks, read books by authors we admire—and as we do, *it gradually becomes easier,* and we feel a sense of readiness that we didn't feel at first.

Limiting Belief #3: I Don't Know Where to Start

Start anywhere. Start by writing about a tulip or a turnip or a tourniquet. It will all lead you to the same place—deeper into the creative process. All roads lead to that place, so long as you are putting one word after another. Give yourself permission to write about anything. Write about the candle burning on your desk (and if there is no candle, go fetch one, light it, and write about it—no excuses). Write about what you see outside a nearby window (and if you don't see anything of interest, close your eyes for five minutes, then open them, and try again). Write about what you dreamt last night (and if you don't remember, then take a notebook to bed with you tonight, and sleep with a pen under your pillow).

It doesn't matter where we start, because where we start is never where we'll end up. Writing takes us to places we aren't expecting to go. It teaches us things we aren't expecting to learn. We don't have to know anything at the outset. We just have to be courageous, and take the first step, at which point the rest of the path will unfold in front of us.

Limiting Belief #4: I'm Not a Creative Person

Brace yourself for this. You are a creative person, and your entire life is an expression of your creativity. In each moment, including this one, you are creatively expressing yourself in some capacity: each time you get dressed in the morning, each time you decide what you're going to eat, each time you have a conversation with someone, each time you express an opinion, each time you read a page in a book and digest its meaning. What do you think all of that is, if not your creativity, your uniqueness, your originality? When you show up to writing or art or life, you are being creative simply by *being*. Your energy, your magnetism, your experiences, your spirit show up with you everywhere you go. There is nothing you have to do, but *be*, and by *being* your creativity shines through.

The Easy Way and the Hard Way

As we become more engaged in the writing process, we learn that there is an easy way and a hard way to write. We take the hard way when we insist on being in control. We write the stories we think we should write. We listen to the voice in our head instead of the voice in our heart. We pressure ourselves to make progress. We take the easy way by releasing our expectations and allowing ourselves to simply be where we are. We write what we feel compelled to write. We let go of everything that weighs on us—the pressure we put on ourselves, the deadlines and due dates, even our vision of what we want the work to become. As our faith in the process grows, we begin to let down our guard and let go of control. *This letting down and letting go of what we think we should write is essential.* It's only then, when we are wide open without expectations, that we can fully receive the writing that wants to come through. It will come from some deep and mysterious place within us, from the furthest corners of our subconscious.

The Mistake Artists Make

The mistake I see artists make again and again when they set out to pursue their creative passion is that they give it too much power over themselves. In the back of their minds they think: *This is what my purpose is. This is how I'm going to make the greatest difference with my life. This is how I'm going to change the world.* On top of this, they also want it to become their full-time career and their sole source of income. They want it to catapult them from where they are now to where they've always dreamed they would be.

They create a vision so big and make it all dependent upon their ability to master their creative passion and become the best writer / singer / painter / musician / dancer / teacher they can be. That's a lot of pressure. No wonder so many people are afraid to take the first step, because the distance from where they are now to where they want to go is too great a leap. They become paralyzed in place because the chasm in front of them is too large to cross, so what's the point in even trying? This is the lesson I want to impart when it comes to pursuing your creative passion: *Do not make your creative passion contingent upon results. Write, sing, paint, make music, dance, teach for the sheer joy of it.* This is the only way you will have the courage to pursue it. Fall in love with the process first, without worrying about where it will lead you.

Giving Our Soul Permission to Speak

Wanting to make art but not doing it is painful. We feel the desire burning inside us, but fear holds us back. *What if we aren't good enough? What if we waste our time? What will other people think?* This fear is present in all artists. With creation comes risk—there's no denying it. When we create art, we are stepping into the unknown where anything can happen. But I have learned that our fear is greatest when we are standing on the outside, looking in. It's the fear of starting that paralyzes us. Once we start, we stop worrying about "what if," and we begin moving with the possibilities that appear before us. When we start writing, all the anxiety we felt about not writing comes to rest. There is a sense of ease, a feeling of peace. We are where we want to be, doing what we want to be doing. At that point, it doesn't matter whether we are doing it well, or where it leads, or what anyone else thinks... *all that matters is that we are giving our soul permission to speak.*

The Narrow Definition of Success

Let's talk about failure. The belief in failure only exists when we define the opposite of it, success, as a single pointed destination. Success is... a million dollars in the bank. Success is... a family with two kids. Success is... a bestselling book. Of course failure exists if our definition of success is so narrowly defined, because anything that falls outside of it is seen as a failure to reach our goal.

But what if we change our definition of success from a single pointed destination to the path of self-discovery that leads us there? Then failure ceases to exist. It no longer matters what we are working toward (that will be different for every one of us); what matters is how we view what we are working toward, and we can choose to view it as an opportunity to know ourselves more deeply. We can continuously be asking ourselves, *who am I capable of becoming through this process of... making a million dollars, having a family and two kids, writing a bestselling book?* When we redefine success as the path of self-discovery that leads to the goal, instead of the goal itself, we will never fail, so long as we are learning and growing along the way.

Actively Living Our Purpose

When we feel unfulfilled in our lives, it's often because we are not moving in the direction of what we want; we are not taking action toward it. I believe that unhappiness stems from not doing the work we have come to this earth to do. It has little to do with whether we are successful or make a lot of money or have nice things. *It has to do with actively living our purpose*, which goes much deeper than success or money or things. When we are actively living our purpose, that is when we find true happiness. Getting there doesn't have to be hard. Start a morning routine. Wake up each morning, and reach for what you love, for what makes you who you are—a journal, a paintbrush, a camera, a guitar. It's about living what's in our hearts each day. If it's in our hearts to write, we write. If it's in our hearts to help people, we help people. If it's in our hearts to travel, we travel. It's simple, and it only becomes complicated when we think we must do more. *What's in your heart, and how can you give voice to it each day?*

Successful Steps

It often takes several tries to get where we want to go. It might take ten bad poems to get to one good one. It might take five books to get to one we actually want to publish. It might take writing on a subject for several days to finally get to the heart of the matter we care about. It would be wrong to call these attempts failures just because they don't appear to directly result in success. They are attempts that lead us closer to where we want to go, and anything that leads us closer to where we want to go is not a failure, but a step. Thomas Edison, one of the world's greatest inventors, said of his many inventions that didn't work: "I have not failed. I've just found 10,000 ways that won't work." If we are aware that it takes many attempts to get where we want to go, and we allow everything that happens to teach us something new that adds to who we are or helps us in some way, then we can see every attempt as a successful step—even the ones that didn't work out exactly as we hoped.

The Hours We Spend Writing

There are times when we write for hours, and we come away with little more than a single usable sentence. There are times when we spend days at the computer, and we have little more than a paragraph to show for it. How disappointing that might seem if it weren't for the fact that all of the work we do—*all of it*—serves a purpose. The hours and days we spend writing matter, every last one of them. We may not always see the direct results on the page in front of us, but we will see the results if we look closely at our lives and who we are becoming. The time we spend writing accumulates deep in our bones; deep in the vascular tissue and skeletal muscle of who we are.

If it appears that hours of work have resulted in little more than a sentence, or days of devotion have little to show for themselves, look deeper. Look to the shifts in your perspective, the changes in your attitude, the subtle differences in the way you see yourself and the world. Your physical, spiritual, and emotional makeup is never the same again after you write. Those hours, those days, those years you spend writing are the very *essence* of who you are.

Quieting the Negative Voices

As artists, we are always aware of what's not working. Either our work is lacking cohesion, or it's lacking direction, or we're lacking the clarity we need to finish it. Even when the work is finished, we may still wonder if there were more we could have said, or a better way we could have said it.

In the past, when I was asked about my writing, I was quick to explain what wasn't working. *I've been so busy; I haven't had time for it. I've hit a wall; I'm not sure where to go from here. It's moving slowly; I don't know when I'll finish it.* There was a strength I was lacking that comes from quieting these negative voices that always have something discouraging to say. Since then, I have learned to ignore these voices and listen to a much greater voice instead, the voice that started me writing in the first place—the voice of love. Now, when I am asked about my work, I talk about how happy I feel in the presence of writing, or how much I'm looking forward to sitting down to write in the days ahead, or the progress I'm making on my current project. I give energy to the things that are moving me forward instead of the things that are holding me back.

Reclaiming the Joy of the Process

Writer's block means that we've temporarily stopped listening to ourselves. It shows up as a sign from our subconscious that we have tuned out our inner voice, our intuition. Perhaps we're forcing the work, or we're getting too analytical, or we're so focused on making progress that we aren't enjoying the process anymore. There are plenty of reasons why we might subconsciously choose to put the brakes on our work.

If you find yourself in this place, step back, take a break, and start doing things that deepen your connection to your inner voice. Take walks. Be in nature. Listen. Observe. Remember why you fell in love with writing in the first place. The joy of the process is what must be reclaimed. You won't find it by trying to force what isn't working to work. You'll find it where you least expect it—in the cool touch of the breeze against your skin, the smell of honeysuckle that brings back memories of your childhood, the stillness of the world as the sun sets and the day draws to an end. You'll find it in the simple things... and you just might be inspired to write about them.

The Ups and Downs of Love

Throughout your life, your relationship with writing will change. There will be moments of pure joy, when you'll feel like one with the writing—working in rhythm, in sync, in precious collaborative harmony. And then there will be moments when you'll feel estranged—disunited, in opposition, working against it, if even working at all. There will be times when you'll want to talk passionately about your work, as if you're falling in love with it for the first time. And there will be times when you'll dread the moment someone asks you about it, because you have nothing encouraging to say. The relationship between the writer and the writing is meant to evolve, to deepen. It is meant to be challenging. This is one of the many beautiful aspects of being a writer—the ever-evolving relationship before us and learning how to nurture it through difficult times. My advice is to fall in love with all of it: the good and the bad, the times when everything is working and the times when everything is not, the inspired moments and the blocked moments alike. Because all of it is adding to us, making us better writers and better human beings.

The Challenge

Writing challenges us. It challenges us to know ourselves at a deeper level with every encounter. It does not challenge us by making us broke or unhappy or sick or lonely, because that isn't the purpose that writing serves. If we ever find ourselves in that position, where the challenge of writing is not a challenge we enjoy, then there is something critical we are missing. The purpose of writing is always to empower us—to help us thrive and flourish, expand and grow.

The Creative Edge

We all have an edge when it comes to creativity—a point we are afraid to go beyond. It may be publishing. It may be sharing our work. It may be showing up to the work in the first place. My creative edge stops at publishing. I have spent my entire life writing, but I have yet to publish. If you're reading this right now, it's because I have gone to my edge and pushed past it… finally. I have other edges as well. Vulnerability has been an edge for me. Am I really capable of sharing who I am in such an undiluted way? If anyone reads what I have written, they will see through to who I am. I will have no shield between myself and other people's judgments. Is that what I want? I won't know until I go to my edge and push past it.

I do believe that wherever the edge is, it's important to identify it and start inching toward it. Slowly. You don't have to rush. Start to entertain the idea of publishing if that's where your edge is. Start to share small portions of your work with the people you trust. Start to be a little more courageous. Start to show up to the work for a few minutes each day. Wherever you feel uncomfortable, that's your edge; that's where you have the greatest capacity for growth. I think we have to go for it. How else will we ever know what's waiting for us on the other side?

Deepening Our Faith

It doesn't matter whether you're spiritual or religious or atheist or agnostic, being a writer will test your faith. In the same way that life tests the faith of both the most spiritual and the least spiritual among us, alike. Whenever there is uncertainty, whenever we are asked to turn over control to the universe, as creativity asks us to do, there is a surrendering. We surrender control of how the process will unfold. We surrender control of what will happen once we take the next step. At times, we may doubt that the universe is working on our behalf, because we cannot see ourselves making progress or the magic at work for us on the other side. But remember, it's in these times, when our faith is called into question, that we are offered an opportunity for deepening—deepening our faith in the universe, deepening our faith in ourselves, deepening our faith in the creative process. Every time we are faced with uncertainty, it is an opportunity to explore our faith and come away with a deeper understanding of who we are.

Getting Out of Our Own Way

A friend of mine is a musician, and whenever she has to perform in public, she won't practice for several days leading up to it. Performing in public is challenging for her because she has to be vulnerable with the people she plays with and the people she plays for. The only way that she can bring herself to take the stage and play for a room full of people is to avoid music for days in advance, in order to distance herself from any fearful thoughts that might arise. *Why am I doing this? Is it worth the stress and anxiety? What if it doesn't go well?* If she let herself, she would quickly talk herself out of playing. So, instead, she knows she has to quiet those fearful voices and get out of her own way. For days leading up to each performance, she focuses her energy on other things—she'll paint a mandala or take a hike in the woods or watch movies—anything to distract herself from playing until the time comes to play. Then, when that little alarm goes off inside her head that says, "it's time," she picks up her instrument and takes the stage, because deep down, beneath the fear, she knows there's no other place she'd rather be.

The Life and Death Process

The creative process can seem like an end of the world process, an end of life process. It can seem like we are dying when we are coming to life. Like the birth of a baby or the death of an elderly person, the transition from one life into the next can feel like it's the end—and it is. It is the end of all we know up until that point, but it is also the beginning of a new world we have yet to discover. The creative process ushers us into new, uncharted territory. It's no wonder so many people are afraid to face the creative side of themselves, because they don't know what they will find. But sometimes we have to go through the darkness to get to the light, whether in birth or death or creativity.

Calling on Faith to Guide Us

Fear is a natural part of any experience that challenges us to see the world in a new way. If we don't know where we are going or how we are going to get there, fear will be present because it represents a new path unfolding. This doesn't mean we shouldn't follow the new path, but sometimes we allow fear to hold us back because it feels safer to stay where we are. We delve too deeply into our fear—we listen to it too much; we talk about it too much; we give it too much power, forgetting that *fear is only the entryway to any new experience*. It isn't meant to hold us back; it's simply meant to remind us that we're entering a new world of possibilities. Whenever we feel that fear is holding us back, then we must call on faith. And if we delve deeply into our faith—if we talk with it, ask it questions, and listen to what it has to say, then faith will speak louder than fear. Faith will guide us the rest of the way.

Growing Tired of Commitments

It is nearly impossible to wake up every day to the same commitments we adhered to the day before and not, at times, grow tired of them. There are times when we have to step back, take a break, and focus on something else for the sake of our sanity. We cannot expect to love or appreciate sitting down to write every time we do it. The people who expect to love writing every day for the rest of their lives are in for a rude awakening. As artists, as human beings, there will be days when we wake up and we do not love the life in front of us. That is an essential part of the creative process. We would not choose it if it were easy, if it did not challenge us, if it did not force us to face the darkest side of ourselves.

The Strength of Our Faith

There will be moments when life tests our faith. When we stop believing in God, or come terribly close. At the same time, there will be moments when we question ourselves as writers. When we give in to our fears, our doubts, our insecurities. It comes and goes like this over the course of our lives, but in the end, it's our resolve to keep coming back to writing, to keep coming back to God, *in spite of our uncertainty*, that determines the strength of our faith.

Resilience

What we find, over time, is that every change in the routine, every unexpected detour in the road, every setback, every tragedy, every failure, adds to our resilience.

Practice: Asking the Universe

Before you go to bed at night, ask the universe to deliver you what you need in your sleep. If you already know what you need, then ask for it directly: *Please relieve me of my worry. Help me find clarity. Help me feel at peace.* If you don't know what you need, then ask for it generally: *If there is anything I need to receive, please deliver it to me in my sleep.* Then forget about it—turn it over to the universe. When you wake up the next morning, notice: How do you feel? What did you dream? Did you have any insights? Sometimes it's apparent right away that we received what we needed while we slept. Other times it's more subtle, and we have to trust that it was worth asking for, and ask again and again. This exercise has helped me countless times to call into my life what I need most. The important thing is it acknowledges to the universe, the magic that works on our behalf, that we believe in it; we believe we are not alone; we believe there is something wonderful and mysterious working alongside us, helping to guide us where we need to go.

You can try this exercise when you write as well. Before you begin, ask the universe for what you need: *Please help me get started. Let my words flow effortlessly. Guide my writing in the direction it needs to go.* Then forget about it, and start writing. Turn it over to the universe. When you finish, notice: Did anything come to you? Did you receive anything you asked for? Did anything surprise you?

Curiosity and Self-Discovery

The unknown is the very essence of creativity.
It's where magic, possibility, and discovery exist.
It's where anything can happen—
our potential is limitless.

Great, Big, Wild Truths

When you see young children at play, learning about the world around them, the smallest details reveal their significance—a leaf, a stone, a bug, a blade of grass, a piece of trash, an acorn. They study these objects with fascination, as if they've just discovered the center of the universe.

As adults, instead of bugs and acorns, we get excited about books, food, music, clothes, art. The world we live in seems far bigger than that of a child's, but when we compare it to the cosmos with hundreds of billions of galaxies in the observable universe alone, our world becomes just as small.

Yet, in learning about the tiny details of our world, we are in turn learning about the cosmos. *A writer's job is to explore the tiniest of details and discover the great, big, wild truths therein*—the way a child discovers an acorn and learns that happiness can be found anywhere in nature, or a caterpillar and learns that life exists in all shapes and sizes. We need only to observe the simple things to know that everything is part of something greater.

The Greatest Things

The greatest things in life are those that we cannot make total sense of. There is an element of divine mystery in all of them. They call on us to use our intuition, to trust in the unknown, to explore our faith, to go deep within ourselves to where we are met by something else. The greatest things in life seem impossible to understand—love, death, truth, creation, God—and they are, through our human capacity, but art gives us the tools to explore them deeper. Art explores into the unknown, into the unseen, into the mystery, and it brings back fragments of the divine.

The Magical Unknown

You don't have to know what you want to say in order to sit down at the computer and write. You don't have to know what you want to draw in order to pick up a pencil and start making marks on the page in front of you. You don't even have to know why you want to create. You can leave the reasoning out of it. Art allows us to participate without knowing all the answers because creativity is, by its very nature, a process of discovery. It will lead us. It will show us where to go. It will surprise us and challenge us and teach us things. In the beginning, the unknown may seem terrifying. We may even allow our fear of the unknown to hold us back at first, but over time we begin to see that the unknown is the *very essence* of creativity. It's where magic, possibility, and discovery exist. It's where anything can happen, our potential is limitless. With practice, we can learn to embrace the unknown, because it is continually offering us more—more to believe in, more to hope for, more to imagine, more to explore.

The Freedom to Explore

You never know where a sentence is going to lead you when you start writing it, but you have to start writing it in order to find out. The point isn't to write the best sentence you can write; the point is to write a sentence that reveals new insights you weren't expecting to find. It's like setting off on a new adventure. You might have a general idea of where you want to go and what you hope to gain by going there, but most of the details fill themselves in once you set off on the journey. Isn't that the best part of an adventure anyway—the freedom you give yourself to explore? Leave room for surprises and spontaneity. Begin each new sentence with open eyes, an open mind, an open heart, knowing that it can lead you anywhere.

The Wisdom of the Subconscious

We discover something new each time we show up to create, because somewhere deep inside of us, in the subconscious, where creativity and imagination thrive, we know much more than we realize. *We know the answers to the questions we are asking.* There is an intuitive awareness beneath the surface of our conscious thoughts, and this is where art takes root. When we create art, we are allowing this subconscious part of ourselves to speak, and when it does we often realize what we weren't aware of on a conscious level. Art is a unifier between the subconscious and the conscious. It brings the answers we know deep down inside of us to the surface. A poem or a painting or a song gives structure to the subconscious, it creates a framework, and the conscious mind relies upon this framework to understand the wisdom that exists within it.

There is No Right or Wrong Way

Asking, "What should I do," or, "How should I do it?" implies there is a right way or at the very least one way that is better. Let's consider this for a moment. I've made a lot of decisions in my life, and the beauty about each one is that it has led me to greater clarity. I chose to fall in love, several times, and several times I've had my heart broken—greater clarity about how I want to love and be loved by those in my life. I chose to attend a state university that was too large for me, at times feeling overwhelmed— greater clarity about how I work best: in small settings with small groups of people. I chose to write for most of my life without publishing a single book—greater clarity about who I am as a writer and the kinds of books I do want to publish. And herein lies the beauty of life, love, and creativity: *We emerge from each experience with a clearer understanding than we started with.* And how can anything that gives us more insight, a clearer vision, and a greater sense of who we are, be wrong? It simply can't. There is no wrong decision you can make. There is no wrong step you can take. There is no wrong way you can live or love or create. *So long as you are learning from each attempt you make.* Don't get hung up on what to do or how to do it. Just do your best, and know that whatever you decide, it will lead to greater clarity.

Treating Ourselves Gently

"How badly do you want to know yourself?" That's the question my yoga instructor asked as we were crouched in chair pose during an especially difficult yoga practice. "An advanced practitioner is measured by how intensely they want to know themselves and by how gently they approach the postures," she continued. "The greater your desire to know yourself, the greater your ease and comfort in the postures." This wisdom from the mat has stayed with me over the years. *The more we know ourselves, the gentler we are with ourselves.* Yoga and writing are similar in this regard. They each serve to deepen our understanding of who we are, and once we begin the practice of knowing ourselves, we intuitively treat ourselves with more love, more respect, and more kindness. So, whether we are practicing yoga or sitting down to write, we know to take our time, to trust ourselves, and to do what feels right.

There Are No Rules

The beauty about creativity is that there are no rules. You're free to create however and whenever and wherever you want. Sometimes so much freedom can seem like a scary thing when you don't know what to do with it or where to start. That's why experimentation is an important part of the creative process. We can find what works for us through our willingness to try new things. Ernest Hemingway wrote standing up at the typewriter. Truman Capote called himself a "horizontal author," and wrote lying down. Jack Kerouac wrote by candlelight. Gertrude Stein wrote in the car while her partner ran errands. Agatha Christie came up with story plots in the bathtub. Wallace Stevens composed poems while taking walks outside, and said he enjoyed matching the words in his head to the rhythm of his steps. We have to find what works for each of us individually, because we have unique preferences and tendencies. Try something out and stick with it, until you find something else that works better.

Trusting the Mystery

When we carve out space to create, we do so without knowing what will fill it. We close our eyes, perhaps set an intention, breathe deeply into the stillness, and what happens from there remains a mystery. We can't know what thoughts we will think, what words we will speak, or what we will feel. We can't anticipate where our emotions will lead us. *So we trust*, turning over the outcome to the universe, knowing that everything will unfold exactly as it should. This sense of not knowing what will happen is an essential part of creativity. As artists, we learn to find comfort in not knowing, and we develop a sense of faith that is continuously growing deeper. Each time we step into the unknown to create, we give of ourselves completely. And in doing so, we open ourselves to receive.

Moving Closer to the Source

The closer you are to a flower, the stronger its effect on you. The smell of lavender or hibiscus or honeysuckle fills your nostrils, and you want more, so you breathe a little deeper and lean in closer. Writing has the same effect. You write a little, and you feel compelled to write a little more, and a little more, and a little more. If you feel this pull from writing, strong or subtle, move closer to it. Because the closer to it you get, the deeper in you will go, and you'll find there's no end to where it will lead you.

Searching for Truth

Did you ever play the game when you were a child where you close your eyes and someone hands you an object, and you have to try to guess what it is? You roll it around in your hands. You feel its shape and size and weight and texture. Is it sharp? Does it have rough edges? Is it smooth? Is it soft? Is it heavy? Is it light? Is it round? Is it angular? You smell it. Does it have a smell? What does it smell like? Fresh flowers? Musty wooden box? Scrap of metal? You try to envision its function. Is it some sort of tool? Is it used around the house? Is it for decoration?

When you don't know what it is, you're stumped; your mind is searching, jumping from one unlikely possibility to the next. Then, suddenly, you realize what it is and there's clarity; it makes sense; your mind stops searching and settles in one place, on one obvious answer. *It's a seashell! It's a leaf! It's a tiny statue!* That's what writing is like. It's a constant state of searching, feeling, open consideration for all things, trying to put a finger on something that eludes you, until that moment when it becomes clear. And in that moment, the truth comes into focus, life makes sense, and the world has order and meaning once again.

Telling the Story in Its Truest Form

If there is one thing I know about the universe and this great mystery we call life, it's that we can never adequately describe it. But we can try, and there is nothing more rewarding than trying to describe the indescribable, the magical, the divine, in such a way that brings us closer to it. *As writers, we are not just storytellers, we are translators. We have an obligation to tell the story in its truest form.* How well are we able to choose our words? How well are we able to convey the truth? How well are we able to translate from the intangible to the tangible, from the immaterial to the material, from the spiritual to the physical?

The Freedom Found in Limits

Writing is freeing, but at the same time it is structured. We are free to do what we want within it, but there are parameters. There are guidelines to follow. We are working within a stratosphere. Fortunately, this doesn't limit us as much as we might think, unless we believe we are limited because the earth is round or because there are one-hundred thousand species of trees on the planet and not one-hundred million or because there are only four seasons a year instead of nine or ten. It doesn't limit us unless we believe we are limited by the color of the sky or the temperature of the earth or the number of stars we see at night. There are potential limitations to everything if we look closely, but there are also just as many—and likely infinitely more—possibilities within each of those limitations. There are only 26 letters in the English alphabet, and yet we can spend our entire lives talking and never run out of things to say. We can devote a lifetime to making art, and still never know all there is to know about creativity.

Following the Yearning

Don't go cautiously into writing. You can't write with one foot in the door and one foot out. Write without hesitation, even though you don't know where it will lead you. Be like a traveler who must rely solely on intuition as a guide. Follow even the smallest yearning to go down this path or that alleyway or this side-street, because even the slightest pull in one direction or another is your intuition guiding you, urging you to explore further. Each time you sit down to write, it will be a practice in disarming yourself of hesitation, fear, and doubt, while trusting yourself to follow your yearning where it wants to go. Give yourself permission to take the path that may lead nowhere. It's the only way you will know what lies down that road.

A Glimmer of Light, a Small Opening

I don't think you can wait around for an idea to come to you before you start writing. You have to go looking for it. You have to start writing somewhere, about something, and see what paths it leads you down. Sometimes, when I'm reading a book that I love, I'll think to myself, *but this story feels so complete, the author must have known what was going to happen ahead of time.* Although, I know that's rarely the case. All one needs is a glimmer of light, a small opening in the brush that hints of a path. Then it's up to us as artists to follow it. I would even go so far as to say that every big decision I have made, every great adventure I have been on, every truly wonderful creation I have given birth to, has been prompted by that small opening and a desire to see where it leads. It's our curiosity and willingness to step into that small opening and follow the unknown path, which leads us to new ideas and new discoveries.

Taking Detours in Life and Writing

My strongest writing often comes when I venture to detour from the path I am on. I usually have no plans to leave where I am. The path I am on is beautiful. There are flowers to pick; there are forests to explore; there is nature and wildlife and scenery. I am happy where I am, for the most part. But there is a small part of me that wonders... *what else?* Could there be a different path with different colored flowers? Could there be bigger or smaller forests to explore? Could there be better views elsewhere? A small part of me wonders, and that small, wondering part is enough to guide me down a new path. I'll end up rewriting my work in a different direction. Sometimes I'll rewrite a paragraph five times, because I want to see all the different directions it can take. I want to see what will happen if I change "we" to "you," or if I shift from past to present tense. There are so many possibilities we can explore in our writing, and we can't be afraid to change directions halfway through. We learn by traveling down different paths before deciding on the final one we want to take. Be willing to experiment with this. Write it once, and then write it again five more times. Why not? You may love it the first time, but you may love it even more the next time.

This is the promise that writing makes: *to continuously surprise us.* So, when you think you have reached the end and the work is finished, you may be surprised to discover there's still farther you can go.

The Darkest Days

Where are you right now, and what are you going through? Whatever your answer, bring it into your writing. Point it toward the page, and let it go. You have no idea where it will lead you until you trust it to show you. Sometimes the most painful emotions can lead us to the most beautiful discoveries—about life, art, and the world. But we have to be willing to explore them. We can't sit back and wait for our lives to change before we start doing the work. We have to give it our best attempt from where we are, regardless of where we are. When we look back at our lives, at all we have been through, we want to be able to say, *I took everything life gave me, even the darkest days, and made something beautiful.*

Art Creates the Artist

While we are busy creating the work, the work is busy creating us. We cannot measure our success solely by the work that we create. We must also consider what the work is creating within us. While we are delving deeper into the creative process, going where we've never gone before, exploring new paths, and discovering new ideas, the creative process is delving deeper into us and sculpting who we are—making us more loving, more insightful, more intuitive, more thoughtful, more aware of ourselves and the world around us. Our curiosity is an open door for these gifts to flow through, and each time we show up to create, we open the door wider for these gifts to reach us.

Practice: Dream Journaling

Dreams are stories with characters and setting and plot and dialogue. We create these stories in our subconscious, and writing about them gives voice to our subconscious. The more attention we give to our dreams, and especially the more attention we give to writing about them, the easier it becomes to tap into our creative subconscious.

To practice this: Keep a journal on your bedside table or beneath your pillow at night. When you wake up in the morning, reach for your journal and write down what you remember about your dreams. Be as detailed as possible. Start from the beginning, and work your way to the end, or start from the end, and work your way back to the beginning. I've often written my dreams backwards, starting from the last thing I remember when I woke up. Think about who, what, where, and how. Who was in the dream with you: people you know or strangers you've never met? What was happening: how did the dream unfold? Where were you: somewhere you know or somewhere new and unfamiliar? How did you feel: angry, scared, excited, nervous? Write down as much as you can remember, in as great of detail as you can recall. Then, when you're finished, ask yourself one more question: *What does it mean to you, what's your biggest takeaway?*

The Writer and
the World

At the end of the day,
when all is said and done,
our greatest work of art
will always be
the life that we create.

The Power to Transform the World

Art is one of the most powerful and effective tools we have to transform the world, because of how quickly it can lead us from darkness to light, from confusion to clarity, from ugliness to beauty, from pain to healing.

When we create art, we start from where we are, from what we are feeling, and then we begin to give shape and form and meaning to that feeling. We point it in the direction we want it to go. What reveals itself next is the innate goodness of humankind, because regardless of the starting point, we want art to lead us somewhere meaningful, somewhere empowering, somewhere that casts light on where we have been and what we have been through. We choose art to lead us through the most challenging times because we know it will lead us to the other side.

As long as we have art in the world (and I believe art will continue to exist for as long as humankind continues to exist), we will always have a pathway to light and clarity and beauty and healing. We will always have the power to transform the world and make it a better place.

Doing the Work We Came to Do

There are two beautiful things that happen simultaneously when we do the work we came here to do. The first is that as we delve into the work, we delve into the well of ourselves. Through writing we begin to understand who we are, why we are the way we are, and what we have come to this world to learn. And each time we write, we draw from this well of ourselves, and we realize there is always deeper that we can go—the supply is never-ending.

The second thing that happens when we do the work we came here to do is that we inspire the people around us to do the work they came here to do. It's natural. When we are drawing from our own endless well, the people around us see how we are transformed, and the desire is born to delve deeper into their own wells by doing the work themselves. What we often don't realize is that simply through the act of doing the work—writing our books, painting our world, singing the song that's in our hearts—we inspire more people than we inspire through the finished creation. We inspire more people through our dedication and perseverance and hard work than we inspire through the books or the paintings or the songs that we produce.

Accepting Ourselves as We Are

One of the most difficult lessons to learn on my path to becoming a writer was that I didn't have to write like anyone else or even resemble the writers I most admired. This was a difficult lesson to learn because every time I read a book that inspired me, I thought to myself, *that's how I want to write! That's the kind of writer I want to be!* For years this sort of thinking held me back, because along with it came the realization that I would never write that way. I would never be able to express the same beautiful insights as Mary Oliver, or write with the same depth of understanding as Madeleine L'Engle, or see the world in the same unconventional way as Henry David Thoreau. I had to learn to be good at being myself and seeing the world in my own unique way, which meant giving myself permission to live and breathe and write without the expectation of being different than I already was. I had to learn how to fully accept myself and love myself for who I was—to fall in love with my own thoughts, my own ideas, my own questions, my own answers. And that is something every one of us can learn in order to bring the most of who we are into the world.

Sharing the Love of Storytelling

My mother taught me the sacred art of storytelling through dreams and writing. She used to climb into bed next to me each morning and write down my dreams from the night before. We loved exploring the deeper, underlying meaning of the dream world. What could flying possibly mean? What causes nightmares? Are some dreams premonitions or signs of what's to come? We wrote to answer these questions and to make sense of what our dreams meant to us. Years later, when I was old enough to know that I wanted to be a writer when I grew up, we would sit at the typewriter together and write stories (I dictated, she typed). We wrote children's stories mostly, and then gave them as gifts to teachers and friends and family members on special occasions.

As adults, we talked about writing and poetry and philosophy for hours at a time. We read each other's work and held nothing back; no critique, no compliment, no question was too small to be meaningful. We shared this love of storytelling throughout our lives. Both of us understood that dreaming and writing are gateways— channels between what's real and imaginary, physical and spiritual. Though these relationships between writers are rare, they do exist, and if we can find even one person who shares our love of storytelling, that is an incredible gift.

The Courage to Be Seen

As artists, we get to choose whether to be seen. It's a scary choice to make. If we choose to hide, to write all day in the comfort of our homes and never share our work, we will be safe. We will never have to confront the discomfort of speaking our truth and being judged. No one will know what we are capable of, except the few select people we share our work with. On the other hand, if we choose to release our work into the world and set it free, we risk criticism. There will be people who won't agree with what we have to say. There will be people who won't want to read what we are putting out. At the same time, there will be people who respond in positive ways. There will be people who see what we are doing and feel inspired to dream bigger themselves. There will be people who read our words and realize that they too have a voice they need to speak. There will be people who love or listen or trust a bit more deeply, who shine a bit more brightly, who dream a bit more daringly—all because we took a risk, and allowed ourselves to be seen.

Sharing Our Work

Why is it so important to share our work? Because our work is an expression of ourselves. It's an expression of who we are at the core of ourselves. What do we really think? What do we really believe? What do we really stand for? Our work tells that story. It doesn't matter whether it's seen by two people or two million, as long as we are speaking our voice and being heard.

Seeing Ourselves in Others

I believe that we recognize the same qualities in other people that we possess in ourselves. A kind person recognizes kindness in others. A spiritual person recognizes others who share the same spiritual depth. An analytical person notices when someone is attuned to the same analytical ways of thinking. We are drawn to people like ourselves and instantly connect with them, as if seeing our own reflection in a mirror. This is why the right people are drawn together at the right time, and why sometimes we are seen and other times we are not. This is true of art as well. When you put your art out into the world, some people will be drawn to it, and others won't. This has little to do with your talent as an artist, and more to do with who is looking. Some people will see your work, and they won't see themselves in it. Others will see themselves instantly. There is nothing you can do to control this, it's simply how the universe works. Knowing this frees us to release our work into the world and trust that the right people will find it. The people who need to read it, will read it. The ones who can benefit from it, will benefit from it. Simply by being yourself and creating the work you love, you'll reach the people you're meant to reach.

The Love between Reader and Writer

What we see written on the page reveals the inner-workings of the writer's life. Beauty on the page reveals the discovery of beauty in the writer's life. Suffering on the page reveals the challenges the writer has had to face. Love on the page reveals the writer's own dealings with heartbreak and compassion and loneliness and union. So, it's no surprise that when we fall in love with a book, we are also falling in love with the person who wrote that book. It's impossible to love a book or a painting or a poem *fully*, without also loving the artist who created it; without also loving the experiences that came together in the artist's life (wonderful and tragic) to shape it; without also loving the revelations the artist arrived at about life and the world while creating it. We share so much with an artist when we are transformed by their work. There is a bond that reveals itself over time to be much deeper than we first realize.

How the Reader Feels

The most valuable feedback that a writer can gain from a reader is an honest expression of how a book or a story or a poem makes them feel. Do our words ring true in the person reading them the same way they rang true in us while we were writing them? Do our feelings translate? Does our clarity give the reader clarity? Do the answers we've arrived at answer the reader's questions, too?

When the writing is true, it traverses time and space to reach the reader wherever they are in their journey. There are truths about the world, truths about the way we love, truths about the things we fear, truths about our deepest dreams and desires, truths about what makes us human, that all human beings feel and share. If a story does its job of expressing these truths, then it can reach the reader anywhere they are, at any point in time, at any juncture in their journey, and it can touch something deep inside of them that makes them feel the way we feel. This is the power we wield as writers. What we are capable of experiencing, we are capable of sharing with others.

Writers' Thoughts on Writing

The main benefit I see to reading other writers' thoughts on writing is that it helps us realize that we are not alone. It was a great comfort to me to discover Madeleine L'Engle's book, *Herself: Reflections on a Writing Life*, because it gave me so much insight into my own life as a writer. As I read her musings, I thought to myself, *that's how I feel! That's what I think! That's how I see the world!* Writing can be a lonely path because we spend so much time alone with our own ideas, but once we realize that there are other writers with similar ideas and insights and challenges, it opens up a new world to us. We can start to form a relationship with these writers the same way we form a relationship with the books they have written. And whenever we are in need of support or encouragement or inspiration, we can simply open up the pages of their books, and we are entrusted with their deepest thoughts.

The Threat of the Artist

An artist is someone who challenges the norm, breaks down barriers, redefines the status quo, sets new standards, questions reality, inspires change, raises awareness, and provokes deeper thinking. This is why artists are seen as a threat in so many places around the world, and still risk jail or exile or even losing their lives. There is no predicting what artists will do; there are no limits to what they can create, and for a government or society that fears change beyond its control, this is a threat. Freedom, creativity, and imagination are seen as threats, because there is no knowing where they will lead.

So, how do we help governments and societies to move beyond their fears? There is only one way that I know—by moving beyond our own fears first. In many ways, it is the same fear of the unknown that afflicts all of us. As artists, we are afraid of what we are capable of creating (just as any government or society is afraid of it). *The difference is that we are willing to explore it, and by exploring it, we are able to see what exists on the other side.* Governments and societies will awaken and heal one person at a time. One by one, as each of us is willing to explore the unknown in our own lives, it will become apparent that we are all artists. We are all contributing in different ways to the same mosaic of life.

Staying True to Ourselves

As an artist, there is an honesty to one's self that we uphold. There is an awareness and understanding that we can only achieve our highest potential when we are doing the work for ourselves first. The moment we start creating for other people, we limit what we are uniquely capable of sharing with the world. If we say what we think other people want to hear, or make ourselves look the way we think other people want us to appear, or create art that we think other people will like, we sacrifice who we are and what we have come to this world to do.

The greatest artists are those who are willing to sacrifice security and popularity and success in order to stay true to who they are. They are the ones who are determined to explore the depths of their own unknown minds and follow their own unanswered questions wherever they lead. They are the ones who value curiosity and self-discovery above all else.

The Risks of Publishing

We write for selfish reasons, but when it comes time to publish our work, we have to be unselfish in order to let the work go free. When we publish, we risk the possibility that our work will be judged or criticized. And along with that comes the possibility that we, too, will be judged or criticized. This is a reality for anyone who has the courage to share their truth with the world. An actor who takes the stage, a musician who picks up an instrument and plays, an artist who adds color to a blank canvas, a teacher who stands up in front of a classroom to teach. There is risk in bringing new ideas to the world, and it is our responsibility as artists to see the value in those risks; to see the potential for what is possible once our ideas take form.

Living What We Love

There is a difference between loving to write and being a writer, and much of my life has been spent exploring that. I have always loved to write, but it has taken me decades to understand what it means to be a writer. What I have learned is this: The love of writing, alone, is not enough. We can love something deeply, more deeply than anything else in the world, but if we don't physically *live* what we love through our thoughts, words, beliefs, and actions, then our love (great as it may be) will never grow beyond us. We may love to write, but unless our love is lived—by physically showing up to do the work, speaking our truth even when it scares us, and having the courage to create what's in our hearts—then we are not writers. Love is the spark of creation; it lights a fire in our hearts, and it drives us to be and do all we want to be and do, but still we must be and do. We must live in line with what we love in order for our love to reach beyond us into the world.

Honoring Our Calling

I have found that the best way to thank the people we love—family and friends who add so much to our lives—is to do the work we are passionate about and honor our own calling. When we have the courage to honor our calling, in spite of fear and uncertainty, we empower the people around us by giving them permission to honor their calling. This is one of the greatest gifts we can share with others, and it is passed on through our own example.

A Gift Greater Than Art

When my mother died, she left behind hundreds of paintings and dozens of notebooks filled with poetry. I kept the boxes of her poems by my bedside and hung her paintings on the wall above my bed. I could feel her spirit close to me. I thought that these were the gifts she had left behind, and I wanted to preserve them. I wanted to turn her poems into books, because they deserved to be read. I wanted to make her paintings into prints, because they belonged in a gallery.

Then it dawned on me one day that her writing and her art were not the gifts she'd left behind; what she left behind was so much greater. My mother lived a life of love. She allowed every poem she wrote and every picture she painted to make her more. Through her creative process, she became more loving, more centered, more intuitive, more honest, more aware of who she was as a woman, an artist, a friend, a wife, a sister, a daughter, a mother. She brought that love and centeredness and intuition and honesty and awareness with her into the world. She passed it on to me, my brother, my father, and everyone whose life she touched. My mother's love was her greatest gift, and it will continue to live on through everyone she ever loved, and through everyone they ever love, and through everyone they ever love, and so on... forevermore.

The Highest Purpose of Art

There are people who sacrifice everything for their art—their happiness, their marriage, their friendships, their health—and for what? So that perhaps, if they're extremely lucky, millions of people will look admiringly upon their work and say what a great artist they were? What a difference they made in the world?

I believe that far more important than the work itself is who we become through the process of creating the work. Does it add to who we are? Does it add to our happiness? Our joy? Our relationships with others? We can leave behind great work—books and paintings and music and inventions that change the way future generations live in the world—but it will always pale in comparison to what we leave behind through the lives that we directly touch. *The most profound gift that we can leave behind in our absence is love.* That isn't to say don't do the work—please, do the work—just realize that the highest purpose that art can serve is to deepen our human experience of love.

Two Worlds Become One

For a long time, it may seem to others around you that you are not a writer, but rather someone who wants to become a writer, because you haven't published anything, you work a regular job or perhaps raise a family, and you have nothing to show with your name on it that proves your identity as a writer. You might even start to question it yourself. But rest assured, the physical world around us takes a long time to catch up to the world we intuitively know and feel within us. Don't be deceived or discouraged. Don't judge your progress by what you see around you. Just keep doing the work you know to do, and eventually these two worlds will catch up to one another, eventually they will become one.

Surrounding Ourselves with Support

Surround yourself with people who see you for who you are and support the steps you are taking to become a writer. Your progress doesn't depend on anyone's support, but it does help to know there are people in your life who believe in you. I had a whole team of people rooting for me, family and friends who saw the time and energy and love I put into writing. This kind of support grows gradually over time. It's a slow and steady evolution that unfolds when we make our intentions known to the world and act in line with our dreams, in spite of our vulnerability. This is seen by others as a declaration of our devotion, and it's often the most inspiring part of the journey to watch.

What Books Make Possible

I have a few favorite books that I keep by my bedside for inspiration: *Gift from the Sea* by Anne Morrow Lindbergh, *Herself: Reflections on a Writing Life* by Madeleine L'Engle, *Devotions* by Mary Oliver, the *Tao Te Ching* by Lao Tzu. I have a relationship with each of these books. I like looking at them and holding them in my hands. I like knowing they're nearby when I need them. Sometimes, I'll turn to a random page and read a few paragraphs, because it reminds me of what books like these make possible. It reminds me of what writers like you or me are capable of, which is the same thing that Lindbergh or L'Engle or Oliver or Tzu were capable of. We are capable of bringing clarity to people's lives when there is confusion. We are capable of bringing hope into people's hearts when there is sadness and suffering. We are capable of casting light into the world when there is fear and darkness. Books are portals that are capable of transporting readers from one reality into another, and as writers we get to share these gifts with our readers in the world we bring them into.

Teaching Others to Write

I don't believe that you can teach someone how to write. I do, however, believe that you can teach someone how to be a better writer. There is something about writing that is unique to every writer—a style, a rhythm, a voice, that cannot be taught by even the best writing teacher. It is something that we are born with and something that remains with us throughout our lives. It is our spirit, and this is what reveals itself through our writing. So, when I speak of teaching others to write, I'm not implying that I wish to teach anyone how to be a writer. I simply wish to share what I have learned through my own experience in the hope that it might inspire and reassure and encourage someone else who may be on the writing path.

What Is True of Art Is True of Life

I've realized through my own creative process that the lessons we learn on the page, the canvas, the stage, can be applied everywhere in our lives. Some of the most valuable lessons I have learned about faith, honesty, trust, vulnerability, love, devotion, loyalty, and commitment, I have learned through the process of writing. I invite you to look within yourself and ask: *What lessons have I learned through the creative process that have helped me?*

Here are a few of the lessons I have learned:

- Showing up to the work and being present is enough. Whatever needs to happen after that will happen naturally.
- If we trust our intuition, it will guide us where we need to go. It may guide us to difficult places, but it has a purpose and a plan.
- Beauty is everywhere, in everyone and everything. If we are looking for it, we will find it.
- Talking about the things we love does nothing for us; we must put our energy into *loving*. Same for talking about the things we want to do, we must put our energy into *doing*.

- As long as we are learning and growing, then we are doing it right—whatever *it* may be.

What It Means to Be a Writer

I have always felt a deep connection with writing, but I've rarely been able to put my feelings into words, which is exactly what writing this book has empowered me to do. I've learned that whether we write about writing or love or grief or quantum physics, we are deepening our understanding of that topic and many other topics along the way. For me, what initially began as a book about writing has become a book about purpose and passion and perseverance and, perhaps most of all, faith.

When we write, we deepen our relationship with ourselves and the world around us. The best part about finishing a book is that I can say to myself, *I am a better person now than I was when I started it.* I am a little bit more forgiving, a little bit softer, a little bit more understanding, a little bit more honest, a little bit more vulnerable. This is what matters at the end of the day, when all our books have been written, and all our words have been spoken, and all our thoughts have been deeply explored. *Have you become a better person at the end of it?* And if the answer is yes, then you have discovered what it truly means to be a writer.

Our Greatest Work of Art

Writing or painting or singing is only the beginning of what it means to be an artist. The real work begins the moment we step away from it, because that is when we are invited to take all that we have learned and carry it back with us into the world. That is when we can apply what we know on a much larger scale, to a much larger canvas—the canvas of life. We can think and speak and act upon the ideas that we have learned through the creative process *in real life*. That is when we become true artists.

What we stand to gain personally from the creative process is far greater than any single piece of art that we create. And when we take all that we have gained and share it with the world around us through the life that we live and the lives that we touch, that is worth more than anything we can share in a book or a painting or a song. The words we speak each day, the choices we make, the intentions that govern our lives, this is where the creative process comes into play. This is where we have the greatest ability to express ourselves as artists. At the end of the day, when all is said and done, our greatest work of art will always be the life that we create.

A Gift to the World

What you have to offer the world is so great, so unique, so unlike what anyone else can offer, and yet you probably see yourself as ordinary, because you live each day as yourself. It's important to realize this distinction. The way you think about the world, the feelings you have on a daily basis, the beliefs you live by, may seem normal to you (it's what you know so well), but it isn't normal for anyone else living alongside you. If you could see how different you are from everyone else, you would realize that all the life lessons you've learned, all of your experiences, have shaped you into who you are—*and who you are is extraordinary.*

There is something so intrinsically special in the way you see the world, the things you notice, the unique combination of your experiences that form your worldview. Your perspective is unique to you. Your insights are unique to you. There will never be another person to walk this earth who is capable of sharing what you, alone, can share. Embrace this, remember this, act on this. Give in all the way to being who you are—it is *your gift* to the world.

Practice: Writing Prompts

A simple prompt can sometimes open the channels of creativity and help us get started. Starting is the most important thing, because once we start we avail ourselves to new ideas and insights and discoveries. Writing prompts are little instigators that kick us into writing action, and from there we can follow the work in whichever direction it leads. The key is to start with the easiest way in, without knowing where it will lead you. If the prompt is to write about a time you got in trouble as a child, then rather than sit around thinking about every time you ever got in trouble, start with the first thing that comes to mind: "There was this one time when I was twelve years old…" or "I was well-behaved until puberty, then all hell broke loose…" Don't think too much about it. Just go. Write. Move your hand and keep it moving as long as you can. You can use these prompts to help you get started. Or bypass them altogether. Or make up some of your own. Or go straight to writing your book. Whatever you want. You decide. You know what's best, and I can't wait to see what you will create.

Write about:

1. A time you got in trouble as a child.

2. A Thanksgiving you remember.
3. An old friend you've lost touch with.
4. Something you did that took a lot of courage.
5. A trip that changed your life.
6. A memorable first date.
7. Something you regret.
8. Your first kiss.
9. An embarrassing memory.
10. The last big decision you made.
11. Your view on marriage.
12. A secret you've never told anyone.
13. One of your proudest accomplishments.
14. Someone you want to forgive.
15. A time you got rejected.
16. A time you rejected someone.
17. A mystical experience you've had.
18. Someone special who passed away.
19. One of your favorite teachers.
20. A birthday you celebrated as a child.
21. A time you got physically ill.
22. Your favorite book.
23. Your faith.
24. Someone who loves you.
25. A bad habit you want to break.
26. Your favorite food.

27. Someone who bullied you in school.
28. Someone you bullied in school.
29. Growing older.
30. A time you confronted someone.
31. A time you took care of someone.
32. A time someone took care of you.
33. A time you broke the law.
34. A nighttime dream you remember.
35. Your writing practice.
36. The best gift you've ever given.
37. The best gift you've ever received.
38. A secret talent you have.
39. A time you stayed up all night.
40. A relative you've never met.
41. A time you got lost.
42. An object in the room around you.
43. How you celebrated your last birthday.
44. How you want to celebrate your next birthday.
45. A game you used to play as a child.
46. Your first "real" job.
47. Something you're struggling with right now.
48. A miracle that happened in your life.
49. The most exotic place you've traveled to.
50. Something romantic you did for someone.
51. A time someone surprised you.

52. A song your mother used to sing to you.

53. What your grandparents are/were like.

54. What brings you the most joy.

55. An author you admire.

56. Someone who makes you laugh.

57. What you have in common with your parents.

58. How you're different from your parents.

59. Your first casual crush.

60. Your first true love.

61. How your parents met.

62. The day you were born.

63. Your first day of school.

64. Where you see yourself five years from now.

65. A time you overcame fear.

66. What freedom means to you.

67. Your favorite place in nature.

68. Something that scared you as a child.

69. Something that scares you now as an adult.

70. Your favorite time of day.

71. Your best friend.

72. The ways you were creative as a child.

73. The ways you are creative now.

74. A time when your faith was tested.

75. A time you had to say good-bye.

76. What first attracts you to a person.

77. What fascinates you about the universe.

78. How you got your first name.

79. Someone you feel unconditional love for.

80. Your favorite holiday.

81. Your least favorite holiday.

82. A pet you have (or had).

83. What you were like as a child.

84. What you are like now as an adult.

85. A time you or someone you loved moved away.

86. Something you're in the process of learning.

87. A new practice or routine you'd like to start.

88. Someone you love spending time with.

89. A challenging experience that's made you stronger.

90. What you're grateful for.

91. How you want to be remembered.

92. Your favorite season of the year.

93. The home you grew up in.

94. Something you're really good at.

95. Something you wish you were better at.

96. The qualities you value in a friend.

97. The qualities you value in yourself.

98. A time you stood up for yourself or someone else.

99. Someone you'd like to reconnect with someday.

100. Where you want to travel next.

Maca Latte Recipe

Makes approx. 16 oz
Preparation time: 5 min

2c Hot water
4x Medjool dates (pitted)
2tbsp Almond butter raw
2tbsp Pecans
2tbsp Cacao powder raw
1tbsp Maca powder
1tsp Vanilla extract (non-alcohol)
1tbsp Coconut sugar crystals (optional)

Blend on high until frothy. Pour into your favorite mug, sip, write, and enjoy.

Thanks to Theresa and Calvin Curameng for this recipe.

ACKNOWLEDGMENTS

This book would never have been written if it were not for the people in my life who have helped me to become the person I am. And more importantly, I would not be the person I am if it were not for their unwavering love and support of me.

My mother, Joan, thank you for introducing me to heaven at an early age and teaching me life's greatest truths about love, light, faith, and God. We have traveled the abyss together, and we have seen what exists on the other side.

My father, Jack, thank you for being my lighthouse. You've lit the path for me (and our family) my whole life, showing me the true meaning of unconditional love and devotion.

My brother, Jay, we have lived a magical life together that cannot be put into words or told in a story. It is ours, alone, to know. Thank you for sharing this gift with me.

My mentor, Mike Dooley, thank you for believing in me and giving me the opportunity to discover what I am capable of. Your confidence in me has given me confidence, your trust in me has made me trustworthy, and your belief in me has made me a believer in myself.

My designer, Gina Tyquiengco, thank you for the countless hours you worked with me on the layout of this book—for your patience, your poise, and your willingness to see my vision through to the end.

My editor, Nikki Fragala Barnes, whose wisdom is on every page of this book, and without whom this book might not exist. Thank you for entering into a friendship with me that isn't afraid to explore the deepest layers of life, love, writing, art, and spirituality.

And, finally, thank you to all my dearest friends and teachers. You have each given me a gift that I will carry with me for the rest of my life. Thank you for the insights you have offered, the support you have shown, and the love you have given me. My gratitude runs deep.

About the Author

Hope Koppelman has devoted her life to writing as a spiritual practice. Inside this book you will find her most evocative insights on writing, life, and spirituality. She weaves together stories and observations about writing, while examining the writer's role in the world and showing us how and why creativity is essential to life.

Made in the USA
Las Vegas, NV
03 March 2024

86642017R00152